A NATURE JOURNAL

Hudson's "Half Moon"

Walt Whitman's Birthplace

Yankee Clipper

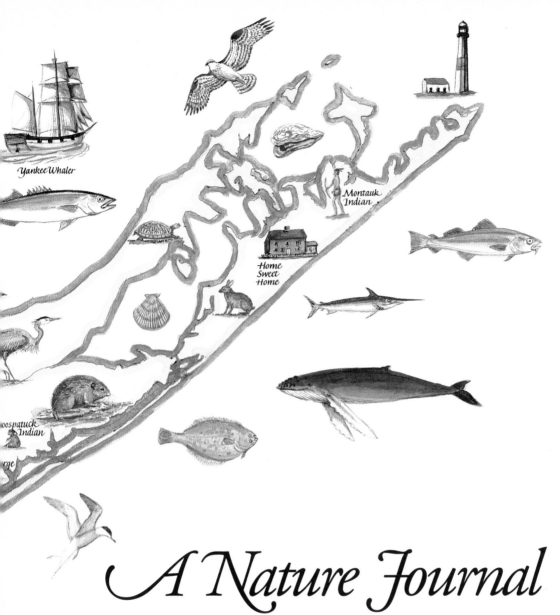

A Nature Journal

A Naturalist's Year on Long Island

Written and illustrated by Dennis Puleston

W. W. NORTON & COMPANY   NEW YORK   LONDON

This book was designed and typeset in Adobe Garamond by Katy Homans with Sayre Coombs.
Copyediting is by Cathy Johnson.
The separations, printing and binding are by Dai Nippon Printing, Tokyo, Japan.
The paper, 86 lb. OK Brite (gloss), is manufactured by Oji Paper Company, Japan,
and is composed of approximately 40% recycled materials.

First Edition

Library of Congress Cataloging-in-Publication Data
Puleston, Dennis, 1904–
A nature journal : a naturalist's year on Long Island/written and illustrated by Dennis Puleston. — 1st ed.
p.   cm.
Includes bibliographical references and index.
ISBN 0-393-03429-1
1. Natural history — New York (State) — Long Island. 2. Wildlife art — New York (State)
— Long Island. I. Title.
QH105.N7P85 1992
508.747'21 — dc20   92-20713
CIP

W. W. Norton & Company, Inc., 500 Fifth Avenue, New York, N.Y. 10110
W. W. Norton & Company, Ltd., 10 Coptic Street, London WC1A1PU

1 2 3 4 5 6 7 8 9 0

To my wonderful family – my wife, children and
grandchildren – and to my many local naturalist friends,
who know, love and work to preserve the best of Long Island
and its natural wonders

CONTENTS

ACKNOWLEDGMENTS

WITHOUT THE ENTHUSIASTIC SUPPORT of Bob Worth, of Worth Publishers, and Joel Plagenz of the Environmental Defense Fund, this book might never have seen the light of day. Elizabeth Scott-Graham, friend and agent, was also an important contributor.

I would also like to pay tribute to the fine editorial, design, and production work of Ed Barber, Sayre Coombs, Katy Homans, Cathy Johnson, and Amy Loyd.

PREFACE

THIS JOURNAL STARTED OUT AS A SMALL PERSONAL GIFT to my family, especially my grandchildren, and to several naturalist friends. We have shared a love for the natural beauties of Long Island and its plant and animal life, and it was my hope that the journal might help remind us all of the wonders of the area, some of which are becoming increasingly rare under the impact of an ever-growing human population. I've organized the material for this book by the months of the calendar year to emphasize that the natural world has much to offer the observer in all seasons—there is as much to see on a chilly winter's day as on a sparkling spring morning.

Long Island is so much more than shopping malls, concrete highways, and crowded towns and beaches. There are still cool woodlands, quiet rivers, salt marshes, overgrown meadows, and rolling sand dunes to be enjoyed by those who have eyes to seek and the desire to learn about the other Long Island, the one that existed long before the first settlers broke ground.

As a resident of the Hamlet of Brookhaven since the end of World War II, I have seen many changes on Long Island. But much is unchanged, and a growing number of dedicated, selfless people are striving to save what remains so that not only we, but also our children, grandchildren, and generations yet unborn, can continue to enjoy the natural treasures of Long Island. In fact, a vital phase of the environmental movement saw its beginning here: In 1967 the Environmental Defense Fund was founded on Long Island, following a successful 1966 lawsuit in which a small group of naturalists and scientists stopped the use of DDT for mosquito control in Suffolk County. The Environmental Defense Fund is now one of the most successful and prestigious of all environmental organizations, its activities ranging worldwide.

If this small book can bring to residents of and newcomers to Long Island an increased awareness of the natural world we share, I will consider it to have succeeded beyond my greatest expectations. Surely this still beautiful area and its wealth of natural resources deserve to be treated by all of us who live here, and also by our close neighbors in New York City, with a full measure of respect, understanding, and love.

DENNIS PULESTON, BROOKHAVEN, NEW YORK, 1992

JANUARY

JANUARY IS SAID TO BE THE CRUELEST MONTH. It is now the depth of winter, with more ice and snow than in all the other months of the year put together, and with temperatures reaching their lowest levels. The deciduous trees stand starkly naked, dormant while conditions are so adverse. Yet nature is far from dead. Around our shorelines the waters are teeming with wintering waterfowl, and although it might seem that all the land birds have moved south, this is certainly not the case. They are simply not as obvious as at other times of the year, as they tend to seek shelter in the evergreens, venturing out only to search for food.

This is a period when it is very important to keep the bird feeders well stocked. A feeder started in the fall has persuaded many birds to stay around when normally they would have migrated southward. By now the birds are dependent on it, and if this vital resource is abruptly discontinued, they may very likely starve to death. Anyone starting

a winter feeding table must maintain it regularly until natural food supplies are available in the spring. In addition to the seeds specially packaged for birds, which are available in most food stores, it is a good idea to hang up a suet basket. Robins, catbirds, and mockingbirds appreciate raisins and chopped apples. Blue jays enjoy bread crumbs, and goldfinches require thistle seed.

One very regular visitor at winter bird-feeding stations is the black-capped chickadee. Even in the bitterest weather this little scrap of feathers gives the impression of being cheerful and contented. Sometimes it joins a loose but sociable band of other species—kinglets, nuthatches, brown creepers, and downy woodpeckers—roaming through the woods in search of seeds, insects, and insect eggs. It has no objection to hanging upside down or at any other angle as it feeds. At a feeder, a lump of suet and a coconut hung on a string are chickadee favorites. Sunflower and pumpkin seeds are also

appreciated. The chickadee is innately inquisitive and can be brought within arm's length by sucking on the back of one's hand to produce squeaky sounds, or by imitating its "phe-be" call. It is always ready to establish friendly relations with people, and with a little patience can be lured closer to accept food from the hand, or even from the lips.

But bird banders can testify to another side of this bird's character. When taken from a mist net or trap to be banded, it fights vigorously, hammering at the bander's fingers with a strength that belies its fragile-looking little body. Some banders refer to it as the "fighting Irishman." For such a small bird to be able to survive the rigors of the northern winter is further testimony to its toughness.

To some, bittersweet is an attractive vine. However, to many gardeners it is a persistent nuisance, creating dense tangles that smother other plants. It is also very difficult to eliminate where it is not wanted. But when its orange-yellow capsules split open to reveal the bright-red fruit inside, the vine brings color to the bleak winter vegetation. It can even serve as a substitute for holly as a decoration in the house. Most birds feed on its berries only when other foods are unavailable, so bittersweet remains colorful throughout most of the winter.

On a typically bitter winter day off Montauk Point, with a stiff wind whipping up the sea, and the spray forming a coat of ice on the rocks, one can often hear a most improbable sound offshore. It is a pleasant musical yodeling, as might come from a particularly harmonious pack of hounds. This is the gay conversation of a flock of old-squaw ducks, birds with the appropriate Latin name of *Clangula hyemalis*, "noisy winter duck." They have also been called "organ ducks."

These hardy and playful little visitors from the far north seem carefree as they rise from the sea with great speed—wheeling and twisting like a flock of sandpipers—and then suddenly drop back into the tossing waters. They are so quick that, at the flash of a gun, they submerge and are gone before the pellets even reach them; they can also dive to extraordinary depths—many have been caught in gill nets at 180 feet down. Long before winter is over, the males begin courting, four or five posing in front of the most

Old-Squaw Ducks, male, left

desirable female, with their long, spiky tails cocked as high as possible and their heads pointed skyward. If a fight starts, the female takes to the air, pursued by the rest of the frantic males, leaving the two battlers—who've presumably forgotten about their inamorata for a while—locked in combat.

When winter is at its worst, with icy blasts sweeping down from the north and snow filling the air, flocks of snow buntings ride down on the chilling winds and swirl about our beaches and dunes amid the driving flakes. As these hardy little visitors from their breeding grounds in the Arctic wheel and twist in concert, their brown backs and black-tipped wings provide a pretty pattern. Then, with a sudden swing, they turn and show their white undersides, seeming to vanish in the snow-filled air, only to reappear as their next swing brings their backs into view again. Having made several passes over an area, they glide to earth and begin to feed among the weeds and grasses, running busily

from plant to plant and helping themselves to the ripened seeds. Snow buntings often feed out on the open beach, their extraordinarily acute eyesight picking out the wind-scattered seeds among the grains of sand. As they feed, their sweet twittering calls are heard, giving the impression of complete contentment and good cheer, in spite of the harsh conditions.

It is worth looking over these flocks carefully, as another Arctic bird often joins the group. This is the Lapland longspur, a smaller, darker bird with sparrowlike streakings on its back and undersides.

If you're walking in a grove of conifers during the winter, you may notice a few pine cone scales fluttering down. Look up, and you'll see several finchlike birds climbing among the cones like miniature parrots. These are red crossbills, although only the adult male is red. The female and juvenile are greenish yellow. These wanderers from the northern forests are feeding on the seeds of the cones, which they extract with their remarkably adapted bills. The tips of the mandibles are actually crossed, and when the crossbill inserts its bill into the side of a cone and opens it, the movement tears out the scales and exposes the seed at the base. The bird then seizes the seed with its scoop-shaped tongue. On Long Island, winter invasions of crossbills are very irregular, but when they do occur, look for the birds in stands of pitch pine. Another species, the white-winged crossbill, also visits Long Island occasionally, but not nearly as often as the red crossbill. It has two broad white wingbars, and the male is more of a pinkish red.

The crossbill, like the dogwood (see May), is featured in a pretty religious legend. It seems that the bird did not always have a crossed bill, but when it saw Christ suffering on the cross, it was so moved with pity that it tried to pull the nails out of his hands, and in its efforts its bill became twisted and its plumage tinged with Christ's blood.

If it were not for the man-made rock jetties and breakwaters along the shores of New Jersey, Long Island, and Connecticut, the purple sandpiper might not be a winter resident in these areas. This small, stubby shorebird, which breeds in the Arctic, requires wave-washed rocks for its feeding ground, where it probes for small marine invertebrates among the seaweed and mussel beds. Until rock jetties and breakwaters were built along our shores, this sandpiper, with its highly specialized habits, was not seen south of the rock-bound Massachusetts coast. It is quite tame, and small flocks can be approached

closely, usually at the seaward end of breakwaters at the inlets. A somewhat vivid imagination is required to confirm the origin of this bird's common name, but there is the faintest gloss of purple on the sandpiper's back feathers when seen in a good light. In its spring breeding plumage, however, which is quite different from the winter one, there is not the slightest suggestion of purple.

FEBRUARY

ALTHOUGH THERE IS NO FOUNDATION for the superstition that the groundhog emerges from his burrow on the second day of February, it has become an amusing tradition to watch for its appearance on this date. If the groundhog sees its shadow, the legend says, it will go back underground, spelling six more weeks of wintry weather. But if there is no shadow to alarm it, the groundhog will end its hibernation, signaling an early spring.

Groundhog or not, there are a few reliable signs that spring is not too far away. First, the days are steadily growing longer as the sun climbs higher in the sky. And courtship performances are under way among the ducks wintering in the bays and off Montauk Point. Horned owls have started nesting; their calls can be heard on clear, crisp nights. Willow twigs are becoming tinged with yellow, and pussy willow catkins are swelling. And there's a touch of green from the few grass blades sprouting in sheltered areas.

In places protected from the north winds, the first dandelions are in bloom. This hardy, adaptable plant, a native of Europe, has spread to many parts of the world. Someone with a fertile imagination compared the flower's jagged leaf with the teeth of a lion, hence its name from the French *dent de lion.* Though considered a bane by anyone wanting an immaculate lawn, the dandelion has a handsome flower that makes an excellent wine, and the early greens, before the plant flowers, make a fine vegetable.

One of the most beautiful of Long Island's wintering waterfowl is the elegant little hooded merganser. Unlike the red-breasted merganser that frequents the salt bays and even the open sea, the hooded merganser almost always remains in our ponds and rivers. In February the drake begins courting the female, dashing back and forth, expanding and contracting his fluffy crest, rising on the water with bill depressed, and then rushing at the female as if to attack her. Although the hooded merganser breeds all the way

Hooded Merganser, male, right

from southern Ontario down to the Gulf Coast, there is only one recent record of a nesting on Long Island. This was in a tree cavity at Mashomack, on Shelter Island. It is likely there are other local breeders that have gone unobserved, so naturalists should be watchful. It would be a pleasure to be able to add this lovely duck to the list of regular Long Island nesters.

Next to the mockingbird (see October), surely our most persistent and optimistic songster is the song sparrow. Although it does not sing continuously like the mocker, the song sparrow's short but cheerful notes can be heard at intervals in every month of the

year. The usual seven- to eleven-note song starts with three identical notes, followed by a trilled note, and a series of quick notes run together. The naturalist Henry David Thoreau has given the song as good a rendition as anyone: "Maids! Maids! Maids! Hang up your tea kettle-ettle-ettle!" Perhaps the song is heard throughout the winter because the sparrow generally stays around the territory staked out earlier in the year, and its song is a declaration of territorial rights. However, we like to think the song sparrow is expressing a cheerful outlook on life

even on the bitterest winter day and promising better times to come. At least, the bird seems to sing with even more than usual verve as February draws on.

As soon as the ice disappears from our ponds and streams, the belted kingfisher is back, selecting a perch from which it can scan the water for the minnows and other small fish on which it mainly feeds. On sighting its prey, the bird partly closes its wings and shoots down like an arrowhead, often disappearing into the water completely. If successful, it rises with the fish in its bill, returns to its perch, and turns the prey headfirst to swallow it. If the fish is larger than usual, the kingfisher beats it vigorously against a limb until it is stunned and then gulps it down. The highly territorial kingfisher protects its fishing rights from rivals, its loud, rattling call serving as a warning. Because it nests in a burrow that it excavates in a sand cliff or bank, there are not many suitable breeding areas on the South Shore of Long Island, but the kingfisher is still seen regularly wherever there are small fish for it to catch. It is an odd-looking bird, with its tousled head feathers, oversized head, and undersized feet, but it is a creature of strong character and a welcome addition to our waterways.

Belted Kingfisher, male

Scattered tufts of cottontail rabbit fur are another early sign of the approach of spring. Normally the rabbit is a peaceable creature, but during the mating season the males have many battles. It is remarkable that this sizeable, defenseless creature manages to survive in built-up areas, where it must exist largely in the backyards of urban households. Here it has adapted readily and established a way of life, in spite of dogs, cats, cars, and boys with BB guns. It even succeeds in remaining hidden during the day and then comes out at night to feed.

We have two species on Long Island, the eastern cottontail and the New England cottontail. The eastern cottontail is believed to be by far the most abundant, but the two species are almost impossible to differentiate in the field. The New England cottontail has shorter and more rounded ears and is slightly smaller on the average.

The harbor seal, a regular visitor to Long Island's coastlines during the late winter, can generally be seen at the inlets along the South Shore, in Gardiners Bay, and off Plum Island and Montauk Point. Some years, as many as forty haul out on the sandbars inside Moriches Inlet. The wary seal chooses the more deserted beaches and offshore rocks, and

at the approach of people, slides back into the water. Once there, it obviously feels more secure and raises its head to watch, as it is an intensely curious animal. Some fishermen are prejudiced against seals, though they do little harm to commercially important fish stocks. They were formerly shot, sometimes for so-called sport, but are now protected in New York State and afford pleasure to the many people who see these peaceable animals during the winter.

Toward the end of the month, you'll notice an abrupt change in the starling's appearance. The bird's bill changes color from black to bright yellow seemingly almost overnight, and the light spots at the tips of its body feathers disappear. The plumage then takes on a more glossy appearance, with iridescent patches of green, purple, and blue among the feathers. Soon after these changes, the birds begin pairing off and exploring tree cavities for future nest sites.

A fine day in late February or early March was once described as "bluebird weather" by country folks, but one seldom hears the term now. The eastern bluebird, formerly a common bird of semi-open country, would announce the promise of approaching spring with its soft, liquid warble. Beautiful in appearance, gentle in manner,

Eastern Bluebirds, male, left

and a valuable consumer of insect pests, this well-loved bird, which is New York's state bird, has become something of a rarity in recent years, and a sighting these days is a thrill. Its main problem has been a shortage of suitable nest sites. The bluebird prefers tree cavities, but the more aggressive house sparrow and starling have given it heavy competition since their introduction from Europe. The native tree swallow and house wren also use tree cavities. Concerned bird lovers are building suitable nesting boxes, and these are resulting in a promising comeback for the bluebird. A nesting box for a bluebird should have an entrance hole of 1.5 inches to exclude starlings, and if the box is located at a height of about six feet from the ground, sparrows will be discouraged. Bluebirds normally raise two broods, and it has often been observed that young of the first brood help in feeding the second. For this and many other reasons, the bluebird deserves all the help and protection we can offer.

As noted, the house or English sparrow is an introduction from Europe. The first successful introduction occurred in Brooklyn in the mid-1850s. Introduced to help control insect pests, the house sparrow instead became a city bird. In the days of horse-drawn traffic, undigested seeds in horse droppings became one of its principal foods. Henry Ford, however, put an end to city horses, and so this adaptable and prolific little bird spread out into suburban and farming areas. It required only about fifty years for the house sparrow to find suitable habitats over most of North America. Not a true sparrow, it belongs to the family of weaver finches and has been described as a "feathered rat" and other uncomplimentary terms. As mentioned earlier, the house sparrow often takes over bluebird nest sites with its untidy nests of straw and feathers, and its droppings are often a nuisance. But as a very resourceful colonist, it deserves some grudging admiration, and when free of city grime, the male is quite a smart-looking bird.

MARCH

SOMETIMES MARCH, THE BLUSTERY MONTH, comes in like a lamb, only to remind us later of its unpleasant reputation, as if it were reluctant to allow winter to slide gradually into spring. Yet there are plenty of signs of the coming change in seasons: Buds are fattening, day lilies and daffodils are thrusting their green spikes above ground, and even in the early days of the month, one can hear the loud, cheery song of the Carolina wren: "tea-kettle, tea-kettle, tea-kettle." Cardinals, too, are in song, and the males are pursuing the females and driving rival males out of the territories they are establishing.

Hazel catkins are suddenly several times larger than they were during the winter; they hang down like yellow lambs' tails, and after a few warm days, a flick of the finger will release a small puff of pollen. Yellow and purple crocus are in flower by the second week of the month, and the silky gray catkins of pussy willow are fully developed and dusted with golden pollen.

Carolina Wren

In boggy areas the skunk cabbage pushes up a pointed spike, which then develops into a shell-like spathe. This opens to reveal the curious flower, one of the season's first to attract the early bees and other insects. After a snowfall, the skunk cabbage, by oxidizing

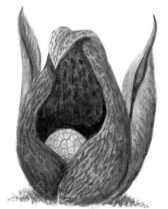

carbohydrates, generates a temperature many degrees higher than ambient and literally melts its way through the frozen ground and snow.

Even while there are still patches of skim ice on freshwater ponds and kettle holes, spotted and tiger salamanders are mating and producing clusters of jellylike egg masses in the shallows. Having reproduced, the adults return to the moist woods, where they spend much of their time under logs and rocks. When the larvae hatch, they have gills and

Spotted Salamander

spend the first part of their lives in the water. Upon reaching a fair size, they lose their gills and tail fins and emerge on land as lung-breathing creatures, continuing to grow until they reach a length of about twelve inches.

After a night of light rain and a rise in temperature, the ground is thickly dotted with tiny mounds of what looks like freshly overturned earth. Close inspection reveals that these mounds, or casts, are the work of earthworms that have risen to the surface after remaining below the frost line for the winter. Moles move upward with the worms, which are one of their principal foods. The ridges known as mole runs indicate their presence, and naturally these busy little animals are not loved by people who maintain golf courses, tennis courts, and lawns. However, moles do perform a useful service by aerating the soil and eating enormous numbers of beetle grubs and other insects. Their spadelike forefeet and strong nails are well adapted for digging. The hairs constituting the velvety fur are all set vertically, so it is just as easy for the animal to move backward as forward. The eyes, mere points, are

Eastern Mole

only of secondary use, but the mole's sense of smell is highly developed and its hearing is very acute. Two species occur on Long Island, the eastern and star-nosed. The latter is extremely rare and in recent years has been found mainly at Belmont Lake State Park.

About half an hour after sunset on a quiet night, the male woodcock begins his spectacular spring courtship flight. He emerges from the moist woods where he has spent the day and alights in an open field or clearing. Strutting like a tiny turkey cock, he utters an explosive, nasal, buzzy sound at intervals of several seconds. Then, like a little helicopter, he suddenly takes to the air in a steep spiral to a considerable height, circles several times, and then descends in a series of abrupt side slips and a final dive that looks as if he will crash. During the final stages of the flight, he produces a string of melodious twitterings that so fill the air they appear to come from every direction. Once he has descended, this strange routine begins all over again, and if the moon is out, it may continue on and off all night.

American Woodcock

Small, round holes in moist earth indicate where woodcocks have been probing for earthworms, which are more than ninety percent of their diet. The birds probably locate the worms through their sense of hearing. The tip of the woodcock's upper mandible is flexible, so it can close on a worm even when the bill is closed at the base. And because the woodcock spends so much of its life probing, it is useful for it to have binocular rear vision; thus its large eyes are located toward the back of the head.

A very harmonious proclamation of early spring is the chorus of the spring peepers. These tiny frogs assemble in moist areas, and when the temperature goes above 48 degrees Fahrenheit, the males inflate their throats into huge bubbles and produce musical calls that have been likened to the sound of many cowbells. Few people have seen these little musicians, for they fall silent when approached. The best way to spot them is to sit quietly at the edge of the pond and wait until they renew their singing, and then try to pinpoint one in a flashlight beam.

Without question our handsomest frog is the wood frog, with its delicate fawn body color set off by the raccoonlike black mask. On warm days in early spring, male wood frogs assemble in woodland ponds. Their continuous clucking calls, sounding somewhat like the quacking of ducks, attract the females, and soon the jellylike egg masses, containing as many as three thousand eggs, are deposited in the shallows. The frogs then disperse back into the moist woods.

The doleful calls that give the mourning dove its name are heard now as pairs begin breeding. The nest is a frail structure of small sticks in a bush or small tree, the two white eggs often visible through its underside. The parent doves may raise as many as four broods during the year, feeding the nestlings a predigested liquid from their crops known as "pigeon milk."

The mourning dove can claim the distinction of being the only North American bird present in every state of the Union except Hawaii. Because it prefers open fields and woodland borders, it is probably far more abundant now than in pioneer days, when so much of the land was covered in forest. Its close relative, the passenger pigeon, occurred in flocks of more than a billion over one hundred years ago, but was massively slaughtered by hunters and deprived of its habitat as forests gave way to settlements and agriculture. Its eventual extinction was due in part to its requirements being much more specialized than those of the mourning dove, which can subsist on weed seeds, waste

grain, and insects. Unfortunately the mourning dove is categorized as a game bird in the South and hunted mercilessly. Thankfully, it is still treated as a songbird on Long Island.

On the bays and rivers the bufflehead are present in large groups, the males displaying to several of the dark-brown females by rearing up and then skimming along the surface to reveal their pink feet. This hardy, dapper little duck derives its name from the male's puffy head, reminiscent of the massive head of the American buffalo. Locally, it is known as "butterball," because of its plump body. Now that they are beginning to pair off, the bufflehead will soon depart for their breeding grounds in the wooded regions of northwestern Canada. Like the wood duck, they nest in tree cavities, often using woodpecker holes.

Of much interest to local fishermen, flounder are now running in Great South Bay, having come into shallow waters to spawn. They take mussel and worm baits. Curiously, canned corn, of all things, will attract them. It's not known how this phenomenon was first discovered, but it is odd that an item so unfamiliar to the fish should be of such interest to them.

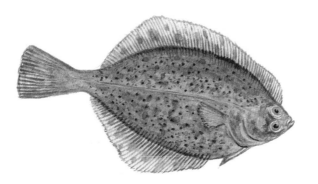

Another sign of the onset of spring, keyed to the appearance of earthworms at ground level, is the arrival of robins in our fields and gardens. Some of the hardier indi-

viduals have been here all through the winter, but naturally there is nothing to interest them on a frozen lawn. They have been surviving in shrubberies and thickets, feeding on fruits and berries. It was once thought that the robin was listening for earthworms when it cocked its head to one side. Not so. Careful studies proved that it is instead watching for the slight stirring of the ground that indicates a worm moving below the surface. This

American bird is not at all like the European robin, but because our bird also has a red breast, it was so named by the early settlers, who were probably homesick for the lands they had left behind.

In addition to the skunk cabbage and some of the early bulbs, one of the flowers of March is the delicate little periwinkle, or myrtle, a creeping plant that forms a carpet on banks and roadsides. An introduction from Europe, it has spread successfully throughout temperate America.

The great horned owl is the earliest nester in the northeastern United States, and by mid-March its young are usually hatched. It does not build a nest but takes over that of a crow, hawk, or other large bird. This splendid bird is an extremely efficient hunter and with its powerful talons can kill a skunk, opossum, and sometimes a domestic cat, although rabbits and voles are its chief food.

By mid-March the first ospreys have arrived, and within the following few weeks they begin to repair their huge stick nests. That we are now seeing these magnificent birds along our shorelines is remarkable; in the fifties and sixties their populations declined so rapidly that many biologists predicted they would disappear from the northeastern United States within twenty years. In the forties, there were about three hundred active nests on Gardiners Island, but by 1965, there were less than twenty and only three chicks could be found. The culprit was DDT, a pesticide commonly used on Long Island then to control mosquitoes.

The use of a broad-spectrum, persistent chemical like DDT to kill mosquitoes can be compared to torpedoing an ocean liner to get rid of the rats on board. DDT and most of the other chlorinated hydrocarbon pesticides persist in the environment and are thus transmitted from one organism to another in a food chain, concentrating in the organism at the top of the chain, in this case the osprey. The chemical interferes with the osprey's ability to produce sufficient calcium carbonate for a healthy eggshell, and the eggs break under the weight of the incubating bird. Thus by the sixties, DDT had reduced the osprey's reproductive success to near zero.

Testimony by a group of local scientists in a 1966 lawsuit put a stop to the use of DDT to control mosquitoes in Long Island's Suffolk County. This suit resulted in the formation of the Environmental Defense Fund in 1967, and this organization's subsequent efforts contributed to a nationwide ban on DDT in 1972. As DDT levels in the environment drop, birds like ospreys, eagles, and peregrine falcons are showing encouraging signs of recovery. There are now well over two hundred active osprey nests on Long Island, including about sixty on Gardiners Island, with an average of 1.5 chicks per active nest.

The handsome mourning cloak is our first spring butterfly and is generally encountered on a warm, windless March day as it flits along a woodland path. This insect will spend the winter hibernating in a tree cavity or an old building. Although quite common here, it is extremely rare in Britain, where it is known as the Camberwell beauty.

One of the first trees to indicate the changing seasons is the red, or swamp, maple. Its small scarlet and yellow flowers open in late March and give rich color to our freshwater wetlands.

The brown-headed cowbird, a small, dark bird, often feeds in flocks around grazing cattle. This bird has extended its range into the Northeast since the clearing of forests and the introduction of cattle. Formerly, it associated with

the great herds of America bison in the prairies. Because these herds were always on the move, the cowbird developed the habit of depositing its eggs in the nests of other birds, taking no further part in the reproductive process. It is now parasitizing many species of birds in the new areas that have opened up for it. Although many intended hosts recognize and eject the cowbird eggs from the nest, other accept them and raise the young intruders. Because the cowbird chick is larger and more aggressive than its nestmates in demanding food, it becomes the sole survivor.

The female cowbird has a remarkably long reproductive period, lasting about two months. On the average, she lays eighty eggs over a two-year reproductive lifetime, and though it has been estimated that only three percent of cowbird eggs result in adults, this is enough to continue the expansion of the breeding range and possibly affect the future of some of the bird species that are victimized. The song sparrow is probably the most frequent cowbird victim. Many flycatcher, warbler, and vireo species are also frequent unwitting hosts.

On warm days in late March or early April, the deep boom of the bullfrog is heard from freshwater ponds. The largest of the North American frogs, the bullfrog grows up to eight inches in length and will swallow almost anything that moves, from insects and fish to mice and even small birds and other frogs. His resonating call is produced by the tympanum, a large, circular organ at the back of the frog's head that looks a little like the head of a drum and serves somewhat the same purpose. The call attracts the smaller female, and mating takes place in the water; the fertilized eggs are enclosed in a jellylike mass, from which the tiny tadpoles will eventually emerge.

APRIL

AS APRIL APPEARS ON STAGE, there are many signs of spring, although a late frost or even a snowstorm are still possibilities. But winter has definitely lost its grip. Leaf buds are opening, lawns are turning green, and some early woodland flowers are in bloom. Wedges of Canada geese and long, irregular skeins of snow geese are passing over, and other smaller migrants are arriving. Insects are stirring, too, and bees are seeking every available source of nectar.

Early in the month the beach plum bushes in sandy areas are a lovely sight with their masses of delicate white or slightly pink blossoms. The abundance of flowers, however, does not necessarily indicate an abundance of fruit in the late summer (see September). The crop yield varies remarkably from one year to the next and may depend upon weather conditions now: If the days are mild and windless, the bees will be able to do a good job of cross-pollination, resulting in a plentiful crop. It is also possible that the plant does not get a plentiful supply of nitrogen in its sandy environment, so following a year with a good crop of fruit, a few years of recovery may be necessary before there is again a sufficient supply. Although beach plums are used in tangy jams and jellies, they can also be incorporated into many other recipes. Wine, desserts, soups, fabric dyes, and even cosmetics are products of this versatile fruit.

The American oystercatcher, a particularly large and handsome member of the shorebird family, is arriving from its wintering grounds further south. Soon after arriving, it begins its courtship and nests in a mere scrape in the sand or pebbles. Since the first nesting was recorded on Gardiners Island in 1957, the oyster-catcher has become increasingly common in our salt bays. Ironically, it rarely touches oysters, its main prey

being mussels, clams, and other marine invertebrates. To obtain a bivalve, the bird inserts the tips of its orange-red bill—flattened in the vertical plane like the blades of a pair of shears—and snips the adductor muscle before the shell closes.

Most shorebirds are protectively colored to blend in with their surroundings. Nature, however, seems to have played a cruel trick on the oystercatcher, giving it a striking black and white plumage and colorful bill. Yet in spite of these apparent handicaps, the oystercatcher survives. But it does not sit tight on its nest like many other shorebirds that hope to be overlooked. At any sign of danger, it sneaks off its nest and then starts fussing with its piping distress calls. Both eggs and small chicks, however, are protectively colored to match their sandy, pebbly background.

When the Pilgrim Fathers had struggled through the rigors of the bitter New England winter, they must have welcomed the flowering of the trailing arbutus in early spring. It is mentioned in loving terms in some of their writings, and it therefore seems appropriate that it is the state flower of Massachusetts. This lowly creeping plant with the leathery, evergreen leaves is found alongside the sandy trails in our deciduous woods, but is rarely noticed until its delicate white to pink five-petaled flowers bloom in April. Do get down on your hands and knees to inhale the exquisite, spicy fragrance of the blooms, but don't interfere with the plant, as it has become rare through overpicking and is now protected by law.

Sometimes in early spring, cardinals and other birds are seen flying against windows, mirrors, hubcaps, and other shiny articles, pecking furiously as if totally demented. What is going on? The answer is quite simple. These are usually male birds fighting their own reflections in the belief that they are attacking an invading rival. During the breeding season birds must have sufficient territory to provide food for the coming family. Hence, the battles for living space, which sometimes result in the complete exhaustion of the contenders.

With the warming of the earth, the box turtle emerges from its underground winter sleep. When alarmed, the reptile can withdraw its head and feet and close them inside the upper and lower halves of its shell by means of a "hinge" on the lower half of the shell. This is a good protection against predatory animals, but not against the automobile. Hundreds of these gentle, harmless creatures are killed every year as they try to cross our highways; many others are killed by brush fires. The male has an orange-red eye

and brighter color on its legs and shell than the female. Its lower shell has a concave depression so that it can fit on the back of the female when mating. Eggs are laid in June, and the young hatch late in the summer but are seldom seen, as they are very secretive.

In recent years, the red-bellied woodpecker, an abundant bird in much of the South, has become an increasingly common breeder in our deciduous woodlands. With its black and white striped back and vivid red head, it is a handsome bird, but misnamed, for neither sex has a truly red belly, only a faint reddish flush that is usually hidden against the trunk to which the bird is clinging. Its frequently repeated call, a rolling "cherr," is very similar to that of the tree frog.

Red-bellied Woodpecker, male

Eastern Painted Turtle

As the water in ponds and streams begins to lose its winter chill, spotted and painted turtles emerge from the mud where they have hibernated. On warm days they sun themselves on half-submerged stumps. But they are always alert and will slide into the water at the approach of possible danger. These turtles feed on aquatic insects and vegetation, seeds, carrion, and small fish. In late spring, the females lay their eggs ashore in light soil.

Around the third week in April, the purple martins arrive. They cluster around the elaborate, multicompartment houses man has provided for them ever since the Indians set out hollowed gourds on tall poles. If all goes well in terms of weather, they will prosper, enlivening the area with their constant, pleasant chatter, and devouring countless numbers of winged insect pests, including mosquitoes. But sometimes cold, damp weather persists after their arrival and flying insects are unavailable. Without food, the martins die off, a tragedy that would have been avoided if the birds had timed their arrival for later in the season, but unfortunately they have not learned to adapt.

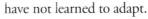

One of the first of the spring warblers to arrive from the south is the ovenbird, but it does not look or behave much like the average warbler: it spends most of its time on the forest floor, walks rather than hops, and has a spotted breast like a thrush. It is quite common, and we are made thoroughly aware of its arrival in late April by its loud, vigorous song, a series of two-note phrases that have been rendered as "teacher, teacher, teacher, teacher, teacher," becoming louder and more emphatic at the end. Once the male has mated, it occasionally gives a wonderful flight song, usually around sundown or during moonlit nights. Quite unlike the normal "teacher" song, it is an ecstatic jumble of wild, ringing notes, poured out as if the little bird were overcome with passion. Sometimes this song concludes with a few of the "teacher" notes as the bird drops back to earth as if exhausted by its efforts. The ovenbird's name comes from its nest, which is built among the dead leaves on the forest floor and is domed over like an old-fashioned Dutch oven.

The killdeer nests on the ground in open fields or even plowed lands, so it must be able to distract predators and lure them away from its eggs or chicks. To this end, the killdeer has become a master in acting. Fluttering in front of the enemy, it drags a half-opened "broken" wing and spread tail along the ground, calling pitifully, but managing to keep just ahead of the interloper. Then, at a sufficient distance from the nest, the bird takes flight. The killdeer places its four pear-shaped eggs with the smaller ends in the center of the nest so that they can be more tightly covered by the incubating bird. If this arrangement is disturbed, the bird soon corrects it. Shortly after the killdeer chicks hatch, they can leave the nest and hide if in danger.

Fowler's Toad, with egg mass

On a warm spring night, the Fowler's toads begin a chorus from the freshwater ponds and ditches where they have come to breed. The males fill their bubblelike throats with air and vibrate them to produce a high-pitched, rolling "song." Whereas frogs lay their eggs in rounded masses of jelly, toads lay theirs in long strings. The tiny tadpoles soon hatch and in a few weeks are losing their tails and developing legs. They emerge on land soon after the development is complete, sometimes in great numbers—which may be a boon for farmers as it was once estimated that toads were worth twenty dollars each to a farmer because of their tremendous appetite for crop-damaging insects. Contrary to an old superstition, people do not develop warts by handling toads, but caution is appropriate because secretions from their skin can be irritating or even poisonous.

On a hot spring day, you might see the least tern alight on the water to wet its feathers and then return to its chicks and shake itself to give them a cooling shower. The least tern is in even deeper trouble than our two other local tern species, common and roseate (see May). Because its beach nests are widely scattered, people are often unaware they are occupying a nesting area, and beach buggy drivers unheedingly destroy the tern's well-camouflaged eggs. It is tragic to see this delicate, dainty little bird now included on the endangered species list.

Least Tern and nest

Red-winged Blackbirds, male, left

When the male red-winged blackbirds arrive here, they begin establishing their territories in the reed beds, but the females do not appear until about ten days or two weeks later.

Ferns do not produce flowers or seeds for reproduction, but instead produce fruiting bodies that give off tiny, dustlike dots known as spores, which are carried off by the wind. Some ferns develop their fruiting bodies on the underside of their leaves, but the handsome cinnamon fern of our moist woods produces separate fertile leaves that stand upright in the middle of green sterile leaves. The rich cinnamon-brown color of the fertile leaves gives this common fern its name. The bud of the fern when it first emerges is a tightly coiled package, like the head of a violin, and is thus called a fiddlehead.

The belted kingfisher, the kingfisher predominant over most of North America, requires a vertical sand cliff or stream bank for nesting. Both male and female alternately dig a horizontal or slightly upward-sloping tunnel that may be anywhere from three to twelve feet long; at the far end of the tunnel is a nest chamber for the clutch of white eggs. The excavation is done mainly with the feet—the kingfisher's middle and outer toes are fused together for part of their length, forming a tough and effective shovel for sand removal—and a kingfisher nest tunnel can be readily identified by the two deep grooves made by the kingfishers' feet at the lower edge of the entrance.

Belted Kingfisher, female

The small green-backed heron arrives from the South and takes up residence along the banks of our creeks and ponds. When startled, it flies off a short distance, uttering harsh squawks of alarm, flops down clumsily at a new perch, and looks around in a seemingly addlebrained manner. As a result, many people dismiss the bird as a gawky, stupid creature. But when it is about its work of catching fish or frogs, it is far from stupid. It patiently stands "frozen" with its neck drawn in, until the moment comes to strike like a flash. Occasionally, it plunges into the water after its prey, kingfisher fashion. It has even been observed using bait: Seeing a piece of bread floating by, the heron deliberately picks it up and sets it in the water where it can reach the minnows attracted to the bait. Unlike most other herons, this bird is not particularly sociable. It generally nests alone, building a flimsy platform of small sticks in a tree close to the water.

MAY

IF ANY MONTH HAS A SMILE ON ITS FACE, it is May. The threat of frost is definitely over. Green shoots are appearing everywhere. Bird migration is at its peak, bringing life, song, and color to woodlands, meadows, and even backyards. On the tidal flats and shorelines as well, birds stop to feed before resuming their long travels northward to their breeding grounds, some as far as the tundra of the high Arctic.

In the shallows, horseshoe, or king, crabs (not to be confused with the larger and certainly more edible king crabs from Alaska) are mating and depositing their eggs in the

sand. When mating, the smaller male is dragged along behind the female, hanging on to her with a special pair of nippers. Shorebirds will find most of the eggs as they probe the sandbars with their long bills, but enough will sur-

vive to maintain the population. The strange-looking horseshoe crab is actually not a crab at all: Its closest living relatives are the spiders, and it has changed very little from the fossils of creatures that lived four hundred million years ago. In spite of being chopped up for bait in crab and fish traps, tormented by unthinking children, and otherwise abused, this harmless creature still survives, an interesting relic from a prehistoric age.

The male three-spine stickleback, like a male bird, is now in his most brilliant colors in preparation for courtship: His lower sides and belly are a rich orange-red, his upper sides iridescent green, and his eyes neon blue. The male, pugnaciously driving away intruders with his sharp spines, builds a tunnel-like nest in the weeds at the bottom of a pond or creek and then attracts a female to it with a strange and elaborate kind of dance, luring her closer until she enters and deposits the eggs, which he then fertilizes. The stickleback does well in salt, brackish, and fresh water and is found from Labrador to Chesapeake Bay, from northern Norway to the Mediterranean, and from China to southern Japan.

Dogwood is in bloom, but it is the bracts, or modified leaves, of the flower that produce the enchanting white clouds through the spring woodlands. The true flowers are the tiny yellowish-green nodules clustered in the center. Legend says the wood of the dogwood was used for the cross on which Christ was crucified. From that time on, the tree has never grown straight enough to serve such a purpose again. But the four bracts are in the form of a cross, and their tips are forever tinged with Christ's blood. A pretty legend, of course, but our dogwood need suffer no feelings of guilt—it is a native American and does not occur in the Holy Land. Its close-textured wood is valued in the manufacture of shuttles for the weaving industry, affording a smooth polish that does not fray the threads. It is also used for golf club heads, mallets, and jewelers' blocks.

Around the second week of the month, a phenomenon occurs that for our local naturalists represents the highlight of the year. This is the passage of the warblers as they head for their breeding grounds, some species to nest locally but most to pass on to the northern forests. Many have wintered as far south as central South America, yet these fragile-looking, five-inch-long scraps of feathers undertake these great journeys on an irresistible impulse, with a few grams of metabolic fat as their source of energy. Their arrival on Long Island is keyed to the availability of an abundant food supply. In most cases, this is the emergence of caterpillars from moth eggs laid the previous year. This high-protein food provides the birds with the "fuel" they require to continue north, mate, nest, and rear young.

The males are now in their full breeding plumage, resplendent in brilliant colors

Blackburnian Warbler, male

Cape May Warbler, male

that seem luminous when lit by the early morning sun. The birds are most active in the early morning hours as they replenish their depleted metabolic reserves after traveling all night. Migration by night makes good sense: Darkness protects the birds from predators, and when their flight ends at daybreak, they can immediately renew their energy by eating.

A wave of warblers usually occurs at the onset of a warm front, with southerly winds assisting them on their flight. A stroll through the deciduous woods on a brisk, sunny morning in mid-May is a memorable experience for a naturalist who has never seen a true warbler wave, when as many as twenty species can be identified. On such an occasion, you'll soon have "warbler neck," an ache at the base of the skull from constantly tipping back your head to aim the binoculars at first one and then another of the restless creatures as they flit through the upper story of the woodlot. Yet the sight of the blazing orange throat of a male Blackburnian or the distinctive cheek-patch of a Cape May makes it all worthwhile. But don't expect musical notes from these birds. Most of their songs consist of insectlike buzzes, chatterings, or lispings. The melodies pleasant to human ears will come from the throats of the wood thrush, northern oriole, rose-breasted grosbeak, scarlet tanager, and other larger birds.

The redstart is probably the most abundant summer warbler in the Northeast, and many individuals remain here to breed in our deciduous woods and shrubberies instead of continuing farther north as so many related species do. A restless bird, much of the time it flutters in the air like a butterfly, then alights with wings half spread and tail fanned, showing off the bright-orange patches. No wonder it is known in Cuba as *la candelita,* the little flame. The female redstart is much more soberly plumaged in olive and yellow. Much of the redstart's

food consists of flying insects, and it darts out after them like a member of the flycatcher family. Also, like a flycatcher, it has a few bristles around the base of its bill, to add to its efficiency as an insect hunter.

There are many species of wild violet, but surely the loveliest is the bird's-foot, so named for the formation of its deeply segmented leaves. It prefers disturbed, sandy, or clay soils and is particularly abundant along the edges of highways, where it lends beauty to areas suffering from roadside litter. There is something deeply touching about the sight of this lovely flower amid discarded beer cans and shreds of plastic.

The terns have arrived on the beaches and sandbars where they form their nesting colonies. These graceful, elegant little seabirds, related to the gulls, feed on small fish, which they capture by diving expertly from on high. Sport fishermen should be grateful to them and help protect them, for terns indicate the presence of game fish by hovering over them and diving at the bait fish being driven to the surface. Unfortunately, sand beaches where terns like to nest are also popular with bathers, picnickers, and beach-buggy drivers, so safe breeding areas are becoming increasingly scarce. Every effort should be made to protect tern nesting sites from early May to the end of August, in particular those of the little least tern, which has been declared an endangered species.

Common Tern

With the rapid increase in gull populations, terns are encountering another problem: Gulls, especially the powerful great black-backed gull, prey on tern eggs and chicks in spite of the vigorous defense put up by the harassed parents.

All 319 species of hummingbird are entirely confined to North and South America, but only one of them, the ruby-throated, occurs on Long Island. This tiny creature, weighing about one-tenth of an ounce, arrives here in May as soon as there are sufficient blossoms to provide it with the nectar it needs for sustenance. Being so small, it loses body heat and energy very quickly, and to maintain itself it must feed throughout the day at fifteen-minute intervals. How then, one might well ask, can it survive through the night, when feeding is impossible? Research reveals that at night the bird's temperature drops from 108 degrees Fahrenheit to about 68 degrees Fahrenheit. Thus, it goes into a sort of nocturnal hibernation that slows down its heart and pulse rates and thereby conserves its energy reserves.

But this brings up another intriguing question that so far has not been answered. During its spring and fall migrations, the ruby-throated hummingbird must make a nonstop crossing of the Gulf of Mexico at its widest span, a distance of more than five hundred miles. Yet a scientist conducting metabolic studies in his laboratory determined that the hummingbird cannot possibly carry sufficient fuel in the form of body fat to fly more than two hundred miles. The hummingbird, however, has not read this report and continues to perform its incredible flights twice each year.

To watch a hummingbird feeding is to realize the amount of energy and agility involved in its flight. Its wings beat so rapidly, about sixty times per second, that they are just a blur and produce the humming sound that has given the family its name. Hovering motionless like a tiny helicopter in front of a flower, the bird extends its tubular tongue and sucks up nectar, also obtaining protein from any insects harbored in the blossom. It then backs off, actually "going into reverse," and darts off to the next flower. It can also move up, down, and sideways with those extraordinarily versatile wings.

During its courtship display, the male zooms up and down before the female in U-shaped arcs, the hum of its wings becoming a loud buzz, with the outer flight feather vibrating at two hundred beats per second.

In 1947, *The New York Times* ran an article reporting the appearance of two strange birds, the great egret and the snowy egret, on our South Shore. Behind this story lay an exciting true-life drama involving man's greed and cruelty, women's vanity, the heroism of a small group of dedicated people, and the brutal murder of one of them. Now that these elegant birds are common in our creeks and marshes, it is worth reviewing their story.

It is difficult to believe that less than a century ago only a few dozen of these birds were left. They had become victims of the dictators of Victorian fashion, who called for the adornment of women's hats with the sprays of feathers known commercially as aigrettes. These delicate, lacy plumes develop on the backs of the adult egrets only during

Snowy Egret   Great Egret

the breeding season. Because the birds nested in close colonies in southern swamps, it was easy for the plume hunters to pick the adults off with their shotguns as the egrets returned to feed their nestlings. In this way, entire colonies were wiped out, with the young perishing of starvation in their nests.

The rapid disappearance of the egrets and other victims of the feather trade aroused the concern of many naturalists, and one of the first acts of the newly formed National Audubon Society was the appointment of several wardens, in a desperate effort to save the last of these endangered species. One of these wardens, a young Floridian named Guy Bradley, was shot to death at point-blank range while apprehending a gang of plume hunters caught with a pile of dead egrets. This murder and the subsequent trial of the killer received sufficient publicity to awaken the nation to the grave situation. Many women, horrified to learn of the slaughter for which they were indirectly responsible, vowed never to wear an aigrette. And, at last, laws were enacted to stop the traffic in plumes.

By this time, however, it was almost too late; the last few egrets seemed well on their way to extinction. But one man determined to dedicate all his energies and material resources to saving the birds: He was Edward McIlhenny, of the wealthy Louisiana family famous for its Tabasco sauce business. With much difficulty, he obtained a few nestling egrets and raised them in a large enclosed area where they could reproduce under almost natural conditions. Slowly the flocks built up to the point where some could be introduced to new artificial colonies along the coast and eventually totally released. Now, as a result of all these dedicated efforts, egrets are familiar birds to us. Surely there could be no more fitting memorial to young Guy Bradley, who gave his life for the cause to which he was pledged.

When the red-eyed vireo arrives in our woodlands and gardens in the spring, we hear its monotonous song all day long: a series of slightly varied phrases of from two to six notes run together, with short pauses in between. These phrases have been interpreted as: "Here I am, can't you see me, Yes, I'm here, I see you," and so on. It suggests a kind of monologue, and the bird has been called "preacher" by country folk. A patient naturalist once followed a vireo through the forest all day long and counted more than twenty-two thousand of these phrases, many of them uttered while the bird was feeding. Surely the naturalist was exhausted by the end of the day, but

not the vireo. Though the mockingbird and song sparrow are our most persistent year-round singers, the red-eyed vireo must be accorded the record for spring and summer.

The nest of the red-eyed vireo is a neat and beautiful little basket suspended by its rim from a horizontal fork of a tree branch. Constructed of strong vegetable fibers, the nest is lined with fine grasses and covered on the outside with lichens, scraps of paper-wasp nests, and shreds of birch bark.

Heronries are now at the peak of activity, with birds incubating eggs and feeding small chicks under crowded conditions in their flimsy stick nests. Most of the colonies are a mixture of black-crowned night herons and snowy egrets, with sometimes a few great and cattle egrets and glossy ibises included. Unfortunately, the birds are easily driven away by human disturbance, so there are fewer heronries on Long Island every year. The black-crowned night heron, as its name implies, is a bird of the night, and this has given it a somewhat mysterious personality. During the day it rests motionless in the dense cover of its roost, waiting until dusk to venture on its night's fishing. It flies with slow wing flaps, uttering an occasional deep-throated "quok" as it heads for some wetland area, where it will hunt for coarse fish, frogs, insects, and occasionally mice and voles.

Black-crowned Night Heron

A heronry is not a place to be visited by the squeamish. The birds are not interested in sanitation rules, and much of the food brought to the chicks is lost in the process of regurgitation. Chicks that tumble from the nests perish and decay, and the air is fetid with ammoniacal fumes. One can quickly become nauseated, but the birds appear to be content except for occasional squawking squabbles between neighbors.

JUNE

JUNE IS A BUSY MONTH FOR MANY BIRDS because most are now caring for chicks. The long daylight hours enable the parents to spend more time foraging for food for their ravenous offspring, and as soon as the first brood is fledged and able to care for itself, many species start on a second family. By this time more of the trees have developed their seeds, and their leaves are fully opened but still bearing that soft, rich green shown when the buds opened in early May.

In moist woods the picturesque jack-in-the-pulpit is flowering. The actual flowers are tiny and well hidden at the base of the spadix, also known as Reverend Jack preaching from his "pulpit," which is the spathe, or hood. Though the root is known as Indian turnip, to taste it would be a mistake, as it will give a sharp burn to the lips and tongue; the Indians ate it only after much boiling.

Around the turn of the century, the great black-backed gull was such a rarity on Long Island that the sighting of a single individual was an exciting event for local naturalists. This largest of the eastern gulls had been overexploited for its eggs and feathers. Now, however, with protection and the easy availability of food at our garbage dumps, its numbers have increased greatly, and there are many colonies of the bird, together with the even more abundant herring gulls, on our coastlines. This majestic bird spends much of its time soaring and wheeling on high and is sometimes mistaken for an eagle. Voracious and aggressive, it preys on the eggs and chicks of terns and other species and is not above taking the young of its own species.

Like gulls, skimmers also nest in colonies, usually along with terns, on open sandy areas. If approached, they fly toward the intruders, their hoarse calls sounding like the barking of dogs. Unlike terns, however, they are not

Great Black-backed Gull

bold enough to actually attack. The bill of the black skimmer appears at first to be a distinct handicap, for the lower mandible extends a good inch beyond the upper one, and both are flattened vertically like the blades of a pair of shears. But the unique bill is a remarkable adaptation, for the skimmer flies low over the shallows in our salt bays with

its bill wide open, the lower mandible cutting the surface as it scoops up its prey, mainly small bait fish and shrimps. As the bird skims—its long, pointed wings held high to keep them clear of the water—its bill occasionally strikes an obstruction, which snaps the skimmer's head down in an odd manner, but doesn't cause it any injury.

We become aware of the large population of spadefoot toads only after an exceptionally heavy, warm rain on a night in late spring. It is then that these curious amphibians, with their catlike eyes and oddly quizzical expressions, emerge from below ground, where they spend so much of their lives, and head for ponds and flooded hollows to mate and lay their eggs in long strings of jelly, filling the air with their barking calls. The spadefoot gets its name from the large horny spurs on its hind feet with which it can

rapidly dig its way backwards into the soil with a corkscrew-like movement of its rear end.

In sandy areas, the formidable snapping turtle emerges from swamps and rivers to dig a hole in which to lay its twenty to thirty spherical eggs, which it then carefully covers and leaves to hatch from the warmth of the soil. When the tiny hatchlings emerge in the late summer, they are on their own, and some will not begin feeding until the following year, spending their

first winter back under the ground. If all the eggs hatched, we would soon be overrun with turtles. However, very few do hatch. Raccoons are expert at locating the nests and digging up the eggs, leaving behind a small depression and the shriveled, leathery shells.

Much has been written about the destruction of baby ducks by snapping turtles, and it is true that snapping turtles are responsible for some waterfowl loss, but waterfowl are a relatively small part of the turtles' diet. They also eat carrion, fish, frogs, and most important, aquatic plants. These turtles should be handled very carefully, as they can strike with the speed of a snake and inflict a serious bite.

Once the marsh grasses are well developed, the best way to encounter the droll little marsh wren (formerly known as the long-billed marsh wren) is to paddle or row quietly along the banks of one of our tidal creeks or the marshy borders of a sluggish river. This nervous little brown bird, clinging to a reed stem with its tail cocked over its back, will eye the intruder apprehensively and then burst into its short, rattling song.

During the breeding season the male industriously builds as many as half a dozen large, globular nests of dried grasses. The female scorns all these incomplete dummy nests and builds her own, lined with feathers and cattail down, in which to lay the eggs.

Possibly these extra nests are a useful ploy: A predator such as a raccoon or black snake might become discouraged after fruitlessly investigating several of them. Or perhaps they are merely a way for the male to work off some of his superabundant sexual energy. He certainly is full of it. He often has more than one mate, and his song is repeated endlessly; as many as fifteen have been counted in one minute. He even sings during the night, especially if there is a moon. A stone tossed into a reed bed where these birds have formed a loose colony will start up a chorus. And sometimes the bird sings as it rises into the air on trembling wings, as if in ecstasy. Because of the dredging and bulkheading of many of our creeks and streams, and the draining and filling of our marshes, this engaging bird has lost much of its habitat.

The dwindling marshes are one of Long Island's richest habitats, and June is the best time for exploring them. The concentration of mammals, birds, reptiles, amphibians, fish, and insects is astonishing. Many bird species nest there, and most of them are feeding young by mid-June. Many strange and beautiful plants also inhabit the marshes, one of the loveliest being the calopogon, or grass-pink orchid. This orchid must be very salt-tolerant, as it can be found even in the upper levels of a salt marsh occasionally flooded by bay waters. Another handsome ground orchid, the rose pogonia, or snakemouth, can be found in the cranberry bog near Riverhead. It is also bright pink, but bears only a single flower on each stem.

Calopogon

Also in bloom now in boggy areas is the curious carnivore, the pitcher plant. Its name comes from its peculiarly shaped fleshy leaves, which grow in a low rosette around the base of the plant. These red-veined leaves are hollowed like pitchers, narrowing at the base. Insects attracted to the liquid at the base of the pitcher crawl in but are unable to push their way out because of the tiny downward-pointing bristles that line the pitcher. Eventually the insects die, drop into the water, and are digested by the plant as a source of nitrogen. The strange-looking, dull red and green globular flower grows on a separate stem.

Whereas these more exotic plants have very special requirements and are consequently rather hard to find, one of our wild roses, the multiflora, seems to be everywhere. Its tall bushes are now covered with masses of small, creamy-white flowers with yellow pistils. This showy shrub, introduced from eastern Asia, is becoming increasingly abundant and is now being planted extensively along our highways. Its dense, thorny growth provides good cover for nesting birds, and the small, round fleshy fruits, when ripe, serve as food.

Two species of cuckoo breed on Long Island during the spring: the yellow-billed and black-billed cuckoos. Their unhurried yet rather secretive, almost furtive, behavior gives them a certain aura of mystery, which is enhanced by their unmusical, unbirdlike calls, quite unlike the clearly enunciated "cuckoo" of the European species, which is reproduced in the famous cuckoo clock.

Yellow-billed Cuckoo

The yellow-billed cuckoo gives a series of clucks that become slower and run down the scale toward the end. The black-billed cuckoo has a long series of soft notes, sometimes running into the hundreds, but without the typical ending of the yellow-billed's song. Old-time countrymen say the calls of both species predict rain; hence the birds are known as "rain crows."

Unlike the European cuckoo, our American cuckoos do not make a general practice of laying their eggs in other birds' nests. They build their own, rather flimsy, nests and raise their families like other self-respecting birds.

Both cuckoos are extremely useful to humankind, as they feed largely on caterpillars, even the hairiest and spiniest of them. Some years ago, when there were many local infestations of the notorious gypsy moth, cuckoos appeared in large numbers and consumed uncounted millions of the caterpillars.

One of the most welcome sounds of early summer is the cheerful call of the bobwhite. Farmers translate it as "more wet" and claim that it foretells rain, an encouraging prediction in times of drought. However, it generally is a rallying call after a covey has become scattered, or sometimes a declaration of territorial rights. The coveys may be made up of several families, and since the broods are quite large, there may be as many as thirty birds in a covey. They sleep together on the ground, side by side in a circular pattern with heads pointed outward, so that if disturbed they can explode in a great flurry in all directions, thus confusing a predator.

Like the young of most ground-nesting birds, the bobwhite chicks hatch with their eyes open, are covered with down, and can run and follow their parents within an hour of hatching. For them to remain around the nest site for long would be too dangerous. In fact, when still quite small the chicks can fly for short distances. Because ground nesters like the bobwhite are subject to high losses of eggs and chicks, both from predators and from chilling after a heavy rainfall, they have to lay many eggs for their species to survive. The number of eggs in a bobwhite clutch is anywhere from twelve to eighteen, and there is more than one brood. The male often takes over the care of the first brood while his mate starts another clutch of eggs, and sometimes two females share the nest, resulting in a huge pile of eggs.

Altricial   Precocial

Now that chicks are emerging from their eggs, it is appropriate to consider the question: Why are some so strikingly ugly to our eyes, and some so appealing? Compare the differences in a newly hatched robin and a baby mallard. The robin is naked, with a scrawny neck topped by a wobbly head, two dark, sightless bulges where the eyes should be, and a gaping red mouth rimmed with yellow. Its internal organs can be seen through its semitransparent skin. On the other hand, what could be more adorable to us than the new-born duckling, or a new-born pheasant or quail, or even a domestic chick? Its eyes are open, it can run and feed itself to some extent, and is somehow "perfect." Each development pattern has its advantages and disadvantages, but obviously both are successful. The ugly robin chick is "altricial," that is, naked and helpless after hatching. The cute duckling is "precocial," meaning it is covered with down and capable of moving on its own soon after hatching.

The altricial chick is born into an elaborate nest, where it can be protected and kept warm by its parents until it has grown feathers. The precocial chick is born into a simple ground nest, or no nest at all, and must quickly learn how to avoid danger. Birds producing altricial young must work harder to build their more intricate nests, but the incubation time for altricials is shorter than that for precocials. All perching birds (passerines), such as warblers, finches, crows, orioles, flycatchers, and sparrows, are fully altricial. Some species, such as hawks, owls, and herons, are semialtricial. They hatch in nests off the ground, but their eyes are open, and they are covered with down.

Toward the end of the month, the native red mulberry tree is laden with fruit. Although red in the early stage, the berries are dark purple when fully ripe. They are sweet and juicy and can be used for pies, jellies, and summer drinks. Naturally, birds enjoy them, too. A related tree, the white mulberry, was introduced from Asia—its leaves are food for silkworms there—and is now well established here. Its berries, which are whitish when ripe, are also very tasty.

JULY

JULY DESERVES TO BE RATED as the beginning of the months of fulfillment. Some crops, like peas, lettuce, strawberries, and spinach, are already being harvested; others are well on their way. Gardens are aglow with flowers, and meadow wildflowers are at their peak, much to the enthusiasm of the butterflies. Bees, too, are at their most active period, gathering nectar for their flourishing broods. Fish are running in the Sound and in the South Shore bays, and blueclaw crabs are large and fat. Most birds are now teaching their young to care for themselves or have already relinquished these responsibilities, and bird song, generally a statement of territorial rights, is diminishing.

The jaunty little goldfinch, however, chooses July or even later in the year to begin breeding. To see its nest is to understand the delay, for the goldfinch uses thistledown as a nest liner and must wait until well past midsummer for this vital construction material. The nest, a beautifully neat little cup, is built entirely by the drab female, while the male sings joyously for encouragement. He is very attentive while she is incubating the eggs and later helps to feed the young. Goldfinches feed mainly on seeds: dandelion, thistle, aster, goldenrod, wild sunflower, evening primrose, chicory, and some garden seeds.

One of the delightful features of a warm, still summer night is the flashing light given off by the lightning bug, or firefly. This insect is actually neither a bug nor a fly; it

is a soft-bodied beetle. The greenish-white light is produced by an organ on the beetle's lower abdomen and serves as a mating signal. Whereas our incandescent electric lamp loses much of the energy it produces in the form of heat, the lightning bug's more efficient lighting system produces no heat at all. The organ consists of fatty tissue threaded with tiny nerves and tubes. The tubes, stimulated by the nerves, introduce oxygen, which combines with chemicals in the fatty tissue to form the cold light known as bioluminescence.

Another feature of a summer dusk is the flight of the bats. Contrary to folklore, bats do not get caught in people's hair, so one shouldn't shy away from observing these small mammals. There are several species on Long Island: little brown, silver-haired, pipistrelle, big brown, red, and hoary. But the only one that is at all common, and the one most likely to be seen on a July evening as it hunts for flying insects, is the little brown bat. In the fall, most of the little brown bats migrate, but a few hibernate here, generally in old barns. Bats locate their prey by echolocation: The high-frequency sounds bats

Little Brown Bat

emit bounce off any nearby object and are then picked up by the bats' remarkable hearing. With this radarlike method, bats can hunt successfully in total darkness.

Sanderlings can be seen along our ocean beaches any month of the year, but in July the first of the breeding population returns from the Arctic tundra on their long southward migration. These little shorebirds are generally in small groups, chasing the receding breakers on twinkling feet, probing for sand fleas and other crustaceans, marine worms, and small mollusks, and then retreating just ahead of the next wave. At this time of year they still have a suggestion of their tawny breeding plumage, but later in the season they become the palest of all the sandpiper family, with a gray and white pattern that matches the sand on which they scamper. As they rise ahead of the beach stroller, their wings show a prominent white stripe. Because they spend so much of their lives on surf-swept beaches, sanderlings are known as "surf snipes."

A handsome flower found in waste, sandy areas, especially near the shoreline, is the horned poppy, also known as sea poppy. An escape from Europe, it derives its name from its very long, curved seed pod, which is divided into three sections. The sap from the plant is a rich yellow.

Another strikingly elegant alien, this one originating in the Orient, is the tawny day lily. Introduced by the early settlers as a garden plant, it has escaped to the wild, and in early summer makes a fine show along our roadsides, although the six-petaled flowers last only for a day. The plant does not produce seeds, but spreads by sending out underground stems, or rhizomes. Note: The fresh buds are delicious when fried lightly in oil or butter!

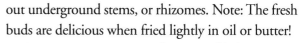

In recent years several species of baleen whales have spent the summer months about twenty miles off Montauk Point—mostly finbacks, minkes, and humpbacks. Now that sightings of these magnificent animals can be almost guaranteed, vessels operating out of Montauk Harbor have been running regular whale-watching cruises for the public. Thus, many people who have never had the unique summer thrill of seeing these gigantic but amiable creatures are now able to watch them close at hand as the skipper gently moves his ship near them. Several species of dolphins, sea turtles, sunfish, and numerous seabirds, including storm petrels, shearwaters, jaegers, gannets, and phalaropes, are often encountered on these cruises. Incidentally, the finback is, next to the blue whale, the largest animal that has ever lived on this earth.

Finback Whale

The round-leaved sundew, like the
pitcher plant (see June), is carnivorous. It
grows in bogs and other moist freshwater
areas. The small leaves that form a rosette at
the base of the central stem are covered with
reddish hairs. At the tip of each hair is a
gland that secretes a sticky juice, which forms
tiny droplets. Insects, attracted to the liquid,
are held until they die and then gradually
digested by the plant.

The bright-orange clusters of butterfly-
weed flowers are now blooming in dry, open
soil, much to the interest of butterflies and
other nectar-seeking insects. Although the butterfly weed is a member of the milkweed
family, its sap is not milky. But the spindle-shaped seed pods do resemble those of the

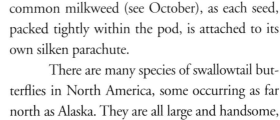

common milkweed (see October), as each seed,
packed tightly within the pod, is attached to its
own silken parachute.

There are many species of swallowtail butterflies in North America, some occurring as far
north as Alaska. They are all large and handsome,
but surely one of the most elegant is the tiger swallowtail, which is a common summer butterfly on
Long Island. It is attracted to bright flowers like
thistles, milkweed, and tiger lilies, sucking their

nectar through a hollow tube, which when not in use
is rolled into a tight coil.

Toward the end of the month, the stately,
straight-stemmed joe-pye weed, from four to six feet
in height, blooms in wet meadows. The large,
rounded clusters of tiny tubular florets vary in color
from dull pink to pale lavender. This plant, a member of the daisy family, is also known as kidney root

and fever weed and was once considered an important medicinal herb. The Joe Pye after whom the plant is named was an Indian medicine man who befriended the early settlers and taught them to use native plants to treat their ailments. Regrettably, we have now lost most of these remedies, but wild plants will always be a source of useful drugs and medicines, and we still have much to learn about them.

The dainty little yellowthroat, a bird of swampy woodlands and tangled shrubberies, is one of several birds starting to move southward by the end of July. Since summer is at its peak, this migration is not, of course, due to food shortage or adverse climatic change. The adult birds, start-

ing second or even third broods, drive away the young of earlier broods. Thus, these juveniles are obliged to migrate quite early in the season. But one might well ask, how do they know where to go? The old theory that more experienced birds show the young where to go during migration has been exploded by banding studies. It seems that birds have almost all the information they need stored in their genes. In other words, they perform most of their functions by instinct rather than by a learning or thought process. The genetic information stored in the DNA molecule is thus transmitted from generation to generation in an amazing, even awe-inspiring, manner.

Juvenile Yellowthroat

What kind of fearsome creature is this? Surely it must be dangerous, one might well think. This is far from the case, however. It is the harmless caterpillar of the beautiful spicebush swallowtail butterfly, which feeds on the leaves of the common spicebush and sassafras. Those false "eyes" are merely a device to frighten off would-be predators. It seems to work in many instances; at any rate, this butterfly is one of the most common members of the handsome swallowtail family.

Snakes have always stirred the human imagination and aroused much unwarranted fear and hatred. It is a pity, because most of them are gentle, and once their initial fear is over, they appear to enjoy the warmth of human hands. They are also beneficial around gardens and farms because they feed largely on rats, mice, and insects. It should be noted that no venomous species remain on Long Island; the last rattlesnake sighting here was in the early 1920s. Our commonest species are the black, garter, ribbon, dekay's, banded water, and hog-nosed, but none of them are nearly as abundant as they were before DDT and other long-lasting chemical pesticides were used on a large scale.

One of our most interesting reptiles is the hog-nosed snake. With its stout body and flat head, it has a dangerous look, and when disturbed it puts on a realistic act, puffing up its head, rattling its tail, hissing, and striking with closed mouth. If this stratagem does not scare off the enemy, it behaves as if it were having a convulsion, writhing about with open mouth and finally rolling onto its back as if dead. If the "lifeless corpse" is turned over, however, it will quickly roll belly up again and continue to play dead until the danger has passed.

Hog-nosed Snake

AUGUST

IN EARLY AUGUST WE SEE THE start of the great annual fall migration as birds far to the north of us begin to move southward toward their winter quarters. Although summer is still at its peak on Long Island, birds breeding farther north are already aware of the pressures of shorter days, deteriorating weather, and dropping temperatures. The first to begin the long southward trek are the shorebirds that have nested

Dunlin, or Red-backed Sandpiper (summer plumage)

in the Arctic tundra. Their reproductive duties have been hurried affairs; most of them were already mated before they reached the breeding grounds, for their offspring must be fledged and ready to care for themselves by the time the migration starts. They must be in top condition to complete the long and stressful journeys ahead of them, some species going as far as the southern tip of South America. To make these long flights, the birds must have plenty of stored energy in the form of fat. As they wander along our coastlines and tidal flats, therefore, they feed intensively on the marine invertebrates now teeming in our salt bays.

Other birds already sensing the first whispers of migration are the barn and tree swallows. They are beginning to assemble on telephone lines and on the heads of *Phragmites* reeds. Like other insectivorous species, they must leave before the autumn frosts deplete their food resources. Remarkably, however, some tree swallows manage to survive during the cold months on the berries of bayberry and poison ivy, and small parties of them overwinter here in the sand dunes.

Barn Swallows

In marshy areas the gorgeous rose mallow, with its large, bright-pink blossoms, is adding color to the reed beds. Like the tropical hibiscus to which it is related, the flower has the characteristic long style tipped with five yellow, buttonlike stigmas. Another name for this spectacular plant is swamp rose.

A rather insignificant but interesting plant of our salt marshes is *Salicornia,* also known as samphire or glasswort. Its fleshy, cylindrical spikes, reaching a height of about twelve to sixteen inches, are now green, but will later turn red. The tiny, barely visible flowers are sunk into the upper joints of the stems. The tender tips of the spikes have a pleasant, slightly salty flavor and can be mixed in salads or pickled in vinegar.

At night the air is filled with the persistent call of the katydids—members of the grasshopper family—as they supposedly sound out their name. The males produce their

song by rubbing together the projecting veins growing at the base of their wings. Since these insects are generally high up in oak, maple, and fruit trees, and their wing covers look like green leaves, it is not often we can find them. But the monotonous calls will be a familiar night sound until the temperature drops.

Just before dusk, the incessant buzzing of nighthawks can be heard as they hawk for flying insects. This bird is not a hawk, nor is it completely nocturnal. It is a close relative of the whip-poor-will and the European nightjar. The nighthawk has recently adapted to an urban environment and often nests on gravel-surfaced roofs. As it hunts for insects attracted to city lights, its nasal calls can be heard over the traffic noise in the streets below. During courtship, following the spring migration, the male nighthawk

makes a loud, hollow booming sound with its wings as it swoops close to the ground. Because its food is almost entirely flying insects, the nighthawk should be afforded every encouragement and protection; nighthawk stomach analyses have revealed more than fifty species of insects—one contained more than two thousand flying ants, and another more than five hundred mosquitoes!

The tall heads of the great reed or *Phragmites* are now ripening into plumes of a deep purple. Somehow this reed, originally from Europe, became established in the New World many years ago and has spread in moist areas to the point where it is now crowding out native plants such as the cattail. It is a strikingly handsome reed, but unfortunately it grows in dense colonies that do not support much wildlife. It does, however, have one beneficial effect: Its tangles of sturdy roots prevent the erosion of waterside banks.

In moist areas the curious plant known as jewelweed or touch-me-not is now in bloom. The orange-yellow flowers, spotted with reddish-brown, hang horizontally on slender stalks. When the seed pods are ripe, a delicate pinch will make them pop open, scattering seeds in all directions. Five spirally coiled valves, like tiny springs, are the plant's elegant strategy for dispersing its progeny. Another odd characteristic is the ability of the leaves to repel water. When a leaf is dunked, it emerges bone dry. Many sufferers from poison ivy claim that rubbing the crushed leaves and stems of jewelweed on the afflicted areas brings the best relief.

Whoever gave the screech owl its unfortunate name had no ear for bird music, for the call is a mellow, tremulous quaver, hauntingly lovely. Soon after dusk, and also before dawn, this small owl is heard. But why do we hear it so often now, but only rarely in the spring? And what is the function of the calling? Some owl watchers believe it is an announcement of hunting territory. Unfortunately, this owl, largely an insect eater, is inclined to swoop at moths illuminated by car headlights and is often struck before it can escape.

The screech owl is either a rich rufous or gray in color. These colors have no connection with age or sex, and an individual owl never changes color. On Long Island, the red phase predominates. Be sure to watch your head in screech owl territory: The adults are very aggressive in defending their young, and many passers-by have had their hats knocked off while walking near a nest tree!

August is an exceptionally active month for the sport fisherman. The main prize now is the bluefish, which occurs in Long Island Sound as well as off the barrier beaches. Voracious feeders, bluefish prey on many kinds of bait fish and in a feeding frenzy will

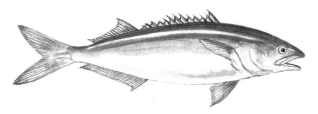

strike at almost anything shiny. Sometimes, in pursuing schools of tinker mackerel, they come all the way in to the beach. There are many reports of bluefish attacking a school of herring or menhaden seemingly for the sheer ferocious sport of chopping them to pieces with their needle-sharp teeth. When hooked, they fight desperately. Young bluefish, known as snappers, are now running in the bays. They afford sport, too, albeit on a far smaller scale. Both bluefish and snappers are prime food fish.

Another tasty wild food of this season is the large and colorful shelf fungus known as chicken-of-the-woods. Found near the roots of hardwood and conifer trees, it grows in a series of overlapping caps. The edible portion is the trimmed margin of the young caps. It is firmer than many other species of edible mushrooms and can be stored in the freezer for future use.

The handsome black-bellied plover, largest of our plovers, is a striking addition to the tidal flats as it passes through on its long migration. On both spring and fall passages, when it travels between its breeding grounds in Alaska, northern Canada, and Siberia, and its wintering quarters in Peru, Brazil, South Africa, and the South Pacific, some birds are in the summer plumage while others are in the drab winter dress. A few individuals even remain here during the colder months. It is a wary bird and keeps well out of gun-shot range, so while the closely related golden plover was almost annihilated by market gunners before legal protection saved the remnants, the black-bellied plover was never

Black-bellied Plovers, summer (left) and winter

seriously reduced in numbers. When the tide is high the plover rests in the salt grass, but as the water recedes it follows the ebb onto the expanses of sand and mud, searching for hoppers, sandworms, mollusks, and crustaceans. Occasionally, it gives its loud, clear, melancholy cry of "toor-a-lee, toor-a-lee."

Cedar Waxwings, male, left

Cedar waxwings are quite unpredictable in their movements. After their rather late breeding season, they become nomadic, forming sociable flocks. Instead of having a regular migration pattern, they appear and disappear depending on the availability of their main foods—berries, fruits, and sap. They can become gluttonous and gorge themselves, but sometimes a row of birds perched on a branch will pass a berry from one to another down the line. When fruit is overripe and fermenting, they have been known to become intoxicated and behave in very unbirdlike ways, falling to the ground and flopping about until sober. Third-year birds develop curious bright-red waxy tips to the shafts of the secondary wing feathers. The function of these decorations is unknown but may help indicate adulthood.

Like other woodpeckers, the yellow-bellied sapsucker has exceptionally stiff tail feathers that serve as a kind of third leg to support it on vertical tree trunks. The sapsucker, however, does not have the typical long, probelike woodpecker tongue that can be extended deep into tree crevices for insects. Instead, it has a fairly short tongue, shaped like a brush at the tip. The bird drills evenly spaced horizontal rows of shallow holes in the bark and returns to these "wells" for sap and the insects the sap attracts. This unique system provides the sapsucker with a rich diet of both plant and animal material at the same feeding site. More than 240 species of trees are exploited by the sapsucker, but fruit trees, apple in particular, are its trees of choice. On warm days, if the sap ferments, the bird may become intoxicated; one naturalist watched an inebriated sapsucker become so befuddled that it landed on his trousers and began climbing up his leg.

SEPTEMBER

BY EARLY SEPTEMBER the handsome orange, black, and white monarch butterflies—also known as milkweed butterflies—have started on their amazing migrations. The barrier beach of the South Shore is one of their major flyways, for here the seaside goldenrod is in bloom, providing its nectar as fuel for the travelers. The butterflies often gather on trees in dense masses before resuming their flight. With their strong wings beating rhythmically, they can attain speeds of twenty-five miles per hour. Upon reaching Florida, California, and Mexico, the monarchs gather in certain groves of trees in such vast numbers that they completely cover the branches. These groves, which have been given protection, are known as "butterfly trees."

Monarch Butterflies and Seaside Goldenrod

When they begin moving northward in the spring, the female monarchs lay their eggs on milkweed plants, and the mated adults die soon after. The larvae feed on the milkweed, the plants' bitter juices making the monarch distasteful prey. Undoubtedly, very few individuals make the complete circuit of more than three thousand miles, and none performs the journey more than once. How, then, do these extraordinary travelers find their way to the same roosts? And how can so much information be transmitted in the genes from one generation to the next and be stored in such tiny brains? We are far from solving such baffling mysteries, but somehow the monarchs know what to do and continue to fascinate us with their wonderful journeys.

By now the beach plums are ripe, and anyone willing to cope with the threats of poison ivy
and mosquitoes can find a rich harvest of this lus-
cious fruit in sandy areas. The dunes behind the
barrier beach are a particularly productive area. It
is surprising that such a juicy plum, a rich purple

when it is fully ripe, can come from such an arid environment. Beach plum jam and jelly
have a special spicy flavor that makes gathering the plums well worthwhile.

With their breeding season over, starlings are forming into flocks of drab gray
juveniles and the more colorful adults. The starling is not a native American, but an
immigrant from Europe. In March 1890, a well-meaning but poorly motivated man
named Eugene Scheifflin released eighty birds in Central Park; the following year an-

other forty were released. When a pair was
found nesting in the eaves of the American
Museum of Natural History building, the
story rated the front page of *The New York
Times*. Now, starlings have spread all the
way across the continent to the West Coast,
where they also occur in large flocks.

In spite of the benefits starlings confer to man by eating insect pests, including
the gypsy moth caterpillar, they are responsible for far more harm than good. They eat
cereal and fruit crops, and during the colder months when they roost on town and city
buildings, their droppings cause much fouling. Yet that is only a portion of the impact
the starling has had in America. It is also having a serious effect on many of our native
birds. Because of its aggressive nature, it can evict other species from the tree cavities
where they nest. Even a bird as large as a flicker can be bullied out of its nest hole by this
insolent intruder. And yet we are forced to admire the starling for its successful invasion
of the New World. Hardy, strong, adaptable, and omnivorous, it is here to stay, and we
must live with it. But it is a striking example of the folly of introducing a foreign species
into a new environment.

Although most members of the shorebird tribe frequent the salt bays and tidal
flats during migration, a few species are more likely to be encountered in an upland environment. Following the potato harvest, pectoral and buff-breasted sandpipers and

golden plovers are seen feeding on grubs and other creatures in the newly turned earth. The buff-breasted sandpiper is surely one of the loveliest and most elegant of all the shore-birds, but sadly it is now among the rarer species because it is remarkably tame and was therefore an easy victim for the market gunners before it was given protection. It migrates all the way to southern Argentina, where it remains until the next spring.

Buff-breasted Sandpiper

The dainty blue flower now blooming along the roadsides is chicory, an escape from Europe. A member of the daisy family, its carrotlike roots—dried and ground into powder—are used as an adulterant or an actual substitute for coffee. The roots contain the carbohydrate inulin, which gives a deep brown color to food stuffs.

The praying mantis, with its forelegs folded as if it were in prayer, may look somewhat pious, but its mating ritual is truly a macabre affair: Once the smaller male is attached to the female's body, she decapitates him, but he continues the act of conjugation for several more days before he dies and is eaten by his voracious mate. Before she dies, she lays several hundred eggs on a twig, which are embedded in a gummy liquid churned into a froth by her abdomen. The frothy material soon hardens to protect the eggs from the rigors of overwintering. Each egg is in a separate chamber, with a hatch through which the tiny young emerge the next spring. Because the mantis feeds entirely on insects and has an enormous appetite, gardeners, in particular, consider the insect beneficial; egg masses are even available from insectariums.

Female Praying Mantis and egg mass

Peregrine Falcon, in a power dive

The autumn hawk migration has started, and one of the best places for observing this exciting phenomenon is along the barrier beach on the South Shore. Hawk species that prey on birds are the most abundant on these flights, since land birds of many species are also using the shoreline as a major flyway. Thus, we see mostly members of the falcon group: kestrels, merlins, and an occasional peregrine. Sharp-shinned and Cooper's hawks are also present, however, and sometimes the odd osprey cruises by, though it does not hunt birds. For a good flight, a brisk northwest wind is necessary. Then, kestrels pass by, heading westward in the hundreds. Sometimes a dozen are in view at one time. Merlins generally dash by at high speed, unless one stops to feed on a victim. During recent seasons peregrine sightings have become more frequent, undoubtedly thanks to the very successful Cornell University project for rearing the young in captivity and then releasing them to the wild.

Many roadside bushes are now blanketed with a climbing vine known as virgin's bower, or clematis. The masses of four-petaled flowers give off a sweet, pervasive perfume. Later, the flowers are succeeded by gray, fluffy plumes attached to the seeds, at which time the plant is known as "old man's beard."

By mid-month the fall migration of many species of land birds is in full swing. The majority travel by night so that they won't be so vulnerable to predation. Having burned up the store of fat that is their source of energy during flight, they seek food as soon as they land at daybreak. Thus, early morning is a good period to observe migrating birds because they are particularly active feeding on the insect and plant life so abundant at this season.

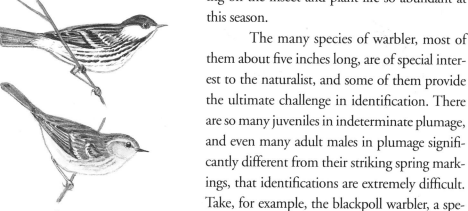

Blackpoll warbler, spring (top) and fall

The many species of warbler, most of them about five inches long, are of special interest to the naturalist, and some of them provide the ultimate challenge in identification. There are so many juveniles in indeterminate plumage, and even many adult males in plumage significantly different from their striking spring markings, that identifications are extremely difficult. Take, for example, the blackpoll warbler, a species that travels all the way between northern Canada and Brazil. How can the bird watcher be expected to reconcile the handsome black-capped bird seen last spring with the yellowish-green bird that appears in September? Many other warblers present equal challenges. That is why the Peterson field guide includes two color plates entitled "confusing fall warblers."

Now that the hickory nuts have ripened, the gray squirrels are busy opening them, and in many cases burying them for future use. Most authorities agree that squirrels are able to recover the nuts they have buried, even when the earth is covered with snow. Although squirrels do not hibernate during the colder months, they become less

active and spend much time sleeping in tree cavities or in bulky nests of leaves and twigs in forks of trees. They have become bold and clever raiders of bird feeders, and it is difficult to devise a feeder that can outwit them.

Whereas squirrels may remember where they bury their nuts, it cannot be denied that blue jays forget where they store many of their acorns. Thus, they can be thanked for some of the stands of oak that grace Long Island. The farmer, however, is not so appreciative of the jay's attacks on corn and sunflower crops. Now that the breeding season is over, the jays gather in flocks and begin moving southward, adding noise and color to our woodlands.

Long before the leaves of oak, maple, and other hardwood trees have started to change color, the ailanthus are already shedding their foliage, but without the dazzling tints  that glorify our fall in the Northeast. Ailanthus leaves simply drop off while still green or else turn a dull brown or yellow, as if the trees were resigned to the coming of winter. When crushed, the leaves have a disagreeable odor, and the soft, pithy wood is of poor quality. In spite of these negative characteristics, the ailanthus is cultivated in China, as the leaves are food for one of the silkworm caterpillars. It is also one of the few trees that does well in crowded cities. Yet, do the good points justify its other name: tree of heaven?

The shorebirds are now heading southward in their myriads. These birds—sandpipers, plovers, godwits, curlews, turnstones, and their relatives—stop off at tidal flats, beaches, salt marshes, and freshly plowed fields to feed on invertebrates, replenishing their energies for the long journeys still ahead. Most of them breed far north in the Arctic tundra, where winter is already setting in. Now, they must move south with their recently fledged broods, some as far as the tip of South America and the Falklands, some to overwinter on tiny islands. In ways that are still mysterious and wonderful to us, they manage to find these specks of land in the vast expanses of open ocean.

Shorebirds: Lesser Yellowlegs, Dunlin, Semipalmated Sandpiper, (left to right)

Naturalists sometimes refer to migrating shorebirds as the wind birds, for they live with the wind, and their melancholy calls are evocative of lonely, windswept shorelines and vast swamplands. Yet, in spite of the birds' stressful lives, their plumage always appears to be immaculate, with never a feather out of place. With their swift, tireless wing beats, these birds are the embodiment of efficient avian flight, as it has evolved from those first clumsy efforts of the Jurassic age.

An historical note involving shorebird migrations: When Columbus was sailing westward in search of the Spice Islands, his men—restless and fearful of falling off the edge of the world—plotted to force him to turn back. It so happened that this was the season of the great fall bird migrations, and when Columbus saw flocks heading south, he changed his course to southwestward because he was enough of a naturalist to realize that these were land birds. It is likely they were golden plovers on a nonstop passage from Labrador or Newfoundland to the coast of South America. By changing his course, Columbus made his landfall on the Bahamas. Had he maintained his westerly course, he would have missed these islands, and in the additional days at sea, there might well have been a mutiny on board and a quite different outcome for the expedition. This seems to prove that it pays to be a bird watcher.

A much neglected but useful fruit that ripens now is the Russian olive, or oleaster, which is found on a handsome shrub with bright-green, pointed leaves. The plum-shaped fruits, about three-eighths of an inch long and dark wine-red when ripe, are in thick clusters along the branches, making very easy picking; juicy, with a slightly tart, astringent flavor, the fruit makes an excellent jelly. It is gratifying to note that many of these fine shrubs have recently been planted along our highways, because although the fruit is largely ignored by humans, it is a great food resource for birds.

OCTOBER

THERE CAN BE NO QUESTION THAT THE MOCKINGBIRD is our most persistent songster. On a fine day in October, it sings with as much enthusiasm and endurance as it did during the breeding season in May. In fact, both sexes sing in the fall, presumably as a declaration of their feeding-territory rights. The mockingbird is also one of our most

abundant songbirds, although it is a relatively new arrival on Long Island. Its population explosion, since the first nesting was recorded in the Mecox Bay area in 1956, has been extraordinary. Once considered a bird belonging to the Deep South, it has been steadily extending its range northward. How to account for this development? Probably the most important factor has been the recent growth in backyard bird feeders, of which mockingbirds have always been steady customers. With their supplies of wild foods thus supplemented, a greater number can survive through the winter. Then, with the establishment of breeding territories in the spring, the younger birds are driven out and thus obliged to open up territories new to the species. Two other southerners, the cardinal and titmouse, are also expanding their ranges northward.

Early in October, seaside goldenrod—the tallest, most abundant, and showiest of all the members of the large goldenrod family—enriches both freshwater and saltwater areas and the outer dunes with its masses of golden-yellow flowers, providing much nectar for insects, including bees. Its honey has a dark color and a strong but pleasant flavor.

Gliding low over our marshes and open fields, the northern harrier, formerly known as the marsh hawk, is moving slowly southward, hunting as it goes. With its long wings held at an upward angle of almost forty-five degrees and its tail fanned, the bird searches tirelessly for the small mammals that are its usual prey, though frogs,

Northern Harrier, or Marsh Hawk, male, left

birds, and large insects are occasionally taken. The great majority of the individuals we see are females, or the young of both sexes, all dark brown above, lighter below. The males, which migrate later in the season, are gray above, whitish below, but male and female alike have a distinctive white rump patch and an owl-like facial disk. Unfortunately, the harrier's low, unhurried flight makes it a handy target for irresponsible hunters, and although officially protected, many are killed each fall in this mindless fashion.

On a bright day in October, a fascinating phenomenon can be observed in the scrub oak and pine barrens that cover sections of central Long Island. This is the mating flight of the male buck moth. The handsome black, white, and red insect emerges from its pupa in the early morning and crawls up the stems of the scrub oak to expand its wings. The female remains on the twigs and releases an airborne sex attractant, or pheromone, that can be detected downwind by the male from more than a mile away. After the mating, the female waits until dusk before making a short dispersal flight and then lands on a scrub oak, where she lays about two hundred eggs in a neat golden ring around a twig. The adults soon die, but the eggs overwinter, and the larvae hatch out the following May. Because the requirements of the buck moth are highly specialized, our local oak and pine barrens are one of the only areas where it occurs in abundance. The days when the matings occur pro-

vide a remarkable spectacle, with hundreds of the moths in the air, each eagerly seeking its mate in the compelling, instinctive urge to perpetuate its kind.

The natty little green-winged teal, our smallest duck, is now moving southward and can be flushed from freshwater ponds and brackish creeks. It is one of the swiftest birds on the wing and has been clocked at more than one hundred miles per hour. In flocks, the birds fly in such close order, collisions seem inevitable. Yet the entire flock twists and turns in unison, as if it were a single organism rather than a group of individuals.

Following an early fall rain, many mushrooms appear in fields and along roadsides. Some of the most colorful are members of the *Amanita* genus. In spite of their handsome appearance, they should be avoided as a source of food at all costs. Some of

them produce toxins that attack the liver, others the nervous system, and they are responsible for more fatalities than all other mushrooms combined. They all have a sac-like cup called a volva, or "poison cup," at the base of the stalk, partially underground.

Fall colors reach their peak in September in northern New England, but October is the best month for enjoying them on Long Island. The maples in particular provide a glorious

display, although if hurricane winds have already bruised and battered the leaves, the anticipated display will be disappointing. The striking colors of a fall leaf are actually a result of its approaching death: The supply of chlorophyll that had previously given the leaf its green color is weakening and undergoing chemical change, and

the red and yellow pigment cells formerly concealed by the abundance of chlorophyll are now exposed. Eventually, all nourishment to the stem ceases and the leaf drops. Thus, the tree conserves its energies until it produces new leaves the following spring.

Hermit Thrush and Tupelo fruits

As the leaves turn scarlet on the tupelo trees, robins and other migrating members of the thrush family gather in the branches, attracted by the tupelo's dark blue, fleshy fruits. Although these berrylike fruits have a bitter taste to us, they are a great favorite with many birds, including ruffed grouse and pheasant. The tupelo—known by several other names, including pepperidge, sour gum, and black gum—prefers wet areas and can be recognized by its corky, deeply grooved, light brown bark and by its branches, which tend to grow at right angles to the main trunk.

Milkweed pods have dried and are starting to split open, releasing their oval brown seeds to the wind. Each seed carries its own parachute, a little puff of silky threads similar to the dandelion's. It is well worth opening a milkweed pod before it has split to see how neatly and beautifully the seeds are packed, each one overlapping the next, like fish scales. The silken parachutes are tightly packed inside the outer layer of seeds, wait-

ing to expand and transport their passengers far and wide when the pod dries and bursts open.

Northern flickers are now migrating in considerable numbers. This large woodpecker has a distinctive white rump patch that catches the eye as the bird flies away. The flash of white would seem to be a handicap, drawing the attention of predators to the bird, but there is a protective device in this bright signal: The enemy's eye is directed to the white patch rather than to the bird as a

whole. As soon as the flicker reaches a perch on a tree limb or on the trunk itself, it folds its wings, covering the patch, and its form blends into the surroundings and thus is lost to the predator. The flicker is the only member of the wood- pecker family that has this white patch, and it serves the bird well, because unlike other woodpeckers, the flicker spends much of its time on the ground feeding on ants. The so-called deflective markings, either in tail feathers or on rumps, occur in many birds that spend much of their lives on or near the ground, including the junco, towhee, meadow-lark, pipit, longspur, mockingbird, whip-poor-will, shrike, horned lark, goldfinch, vesper sparrow, snow bunting, blue jay, wheatear, and mourning dove.

Another Long Island resident uses its deflective markings to confuse predators: The Virginia white-tailed deer, when startled, raises its tail, exposing the large white underside, a vivid eye-catcher. After the deer has run to a safe distance, it lowers its tail and blends back into the shade of the woods.

The chipmunk, alert and active all through the spring and summer, now seems to be busier than ever. At least we are more aware of its presence. Not only is it feverishly engaged in hoarding seeds, nuts, and fruits, it also "chips" incessantly to announce its territory and warn off competitors. And yet, instead of surviving on its stored food supplies during the winter, it disappears into its underground nest and goes into a deep sleep lasting several months. Perhaps it remembers its cache when it awakens the next spring and uses it before there is much food elsewhere.

A faint clamor in the sky from afar tells us that the Canada geese are on the move; when their calls finally fill the air, a wedge of birds can be seen high overhead, as

they head purposefully to their southern wintering grounds. The leader is one of the older, more experienced birds, but because this is the most tiring position in the flock, changes of leadership take place on the longer flights. Communication between the

members of the flock is almost constant, and the musical honking is a sound that has thrilled man through the centuries. The V-formation is the easiest for protracted passages: Each bird has enough room to work its wings freely and yet avoids some wind resistance by flying in the wake of the bird ahead.

The stems of pokeweed have already turned a brilliant scarlet. After several October frosts, the leaves will also produce patches of various tints of bright red, adding their vibrant colors to those of the maples. The juicy fruits, clustered along a slender stem, are a favorite food of catbirds and other species. They turn a shiny purplish black, and it is believed that the early settlers used the juice for writing ink. When the shoots of this handsome plant emerge from the soil in May and reach a height of about ten inches, they can be cooked and served as a very acceptable spring vegetable.

If you stroll through a wooded or brushy area on Long Island, you may be startled by a vigorous rustling in the dry, fallen leaves that suggests the presence of a large animal. But it is probably only the rufous-sided towhee, a small, handsome bird that can create an amazing amount of disturbance for its size. The towhee spends most of its time on the ground, energetically foraging like a miniature chicken for insects, seeds, and fruits in the leaf litter. The bird's song usually consists of three clearly enunciated notes, the first two on a higher pitch than the last, which is drawn out into a medium-pitched trill. The song has been transliterated as "drink your teeeeeeeee," but later in the season the last note is often broken into two, so that it comes out as "drink your whiskeeeee." This bird is also known as "chewink"; both its names are interpretations of its cheerful sounding call note. The female and young have similar markings to the male, but are cinnamon brown where the male is black.

The first wave of white-throated sparrows arrives from the north, and small groups shuffle noisily in the dead leaves, searching for seeds and insects. More waves will follow, and many of the sparrows will remain with us for the winter, sheltering in thickets and brush piles. This bird is considered to be the sweetest singer of all the sparrow tribe, and although we do not often hear the beautiful but melancholy plaint on Long Island, it is worth listening for. It has been phonetically interpreted as "Old Sam Peabody, Peabody, Peabody," or "Ah, poor Canada, Canada, Canada," sung in a thin, high-pitched minor key, with an air of infinite sadness.

In the fall, the woolly bear caterpillar is often encountered rapidly making its way to a hiding place where it can hibernate. If disturbed, it rolls into a tight ball, feigning death. The woolly bear is the larva of the Isabella tiger moth, a rather drab yellowish-brown insect with three rows of small black dots on the body. The history of the caterpillar, however, is far from drab. It seems when early settlers asked the local Indians whether an approaching winter would be mild or severe, the Indians' predictions always turned out to be correct. When asked how they could tell, the Indians explained that the woolly bear was their forecaster. If the orange-brown band around the creature's middle was broad, the winter would be mild, but if narrow, the weather would be severe. And it is a fact that the width of the band varies considerably from one year to the next. Entomologists are endeavoring to test the validity of this phenomenon by averaging the widths of the caterpillars' bands each year and comparing their measurements to the following winter weather conditions. So far the Indians, and the bristly little woolly bear caterpillars, seem to know what they are doing, but it will require many more winters before the results of the study are clear.

Long after catbirds, blue jays, robins, and other birds have raised their young and abandoned their nests, the white-footed mouse, seeking a home for its family, moves in.

Using cattail wool and other plant fibers for a lining, the mouse makes the nest a fairly secure, warm, and comfortable retreat for the coming winter. We don't often see this mouse because it is largely nocturnal, but it is very abundant and adaptable to a variety of habitats. With its large, liquid, night-adapted eyes, neat russet coat, and white belly, it is an appealing little animal, though entomologists have recently determined that it is one of the principal carriers of the deer tick, whose bite can transmit Lyme disease. A program is now under way to leave chemically treated cotton wool in places where mice are likely to find it and use it as nesting material. The chemical in the wool kills the ticks but does not harm the mice.

If you're walking in a dark grove of conifers or other evergreens and find several neat cylindrical packets of fur and bones at the foot of a tree, you'll know an owl has been roosting during the day in the branches above, for these pellets are the regurgitated remains of its prey. Owls swallow their prey whole, and their digestive processes are so efficient that every particle of useful food is assimilated, leaving only a compact, clean, and odorless bundle of fur, feathers, bones, or insect exoskeletons remaining. By examining the bones in an owl pellet, one can identify the creatures the bird has eaten. Gulls, hawks, and crows also eject pellets, but since they are more inclined to tear their prey apart before swallowing it, their pellets are not as informative as those of owls.

Owl pellet

Gull pellet

NOVEMBER

✤

EARLY IN THE MONTH the tiny winter wren arrives in our thickets from its summer home in the moist northern woods. It is always restless, busy searching for insects and spiders and their eggs, usually keeping close to the ground. When disturbed it flits very short distances, scuttling furtively like a wood mouse into dense cover. This same species occurs throughout most of Europe, where it is known simply as "the wren," since it is the only member of the family on that continent, in contrast to the many species we can claim for North America.

As the month advances, the last of the Norway maple leaves come down. They have by now lost most of their brilliant reds and oranges and have faded to softer yellows and browns, in some ways as lovely as the earlier, more spectacular tints. An occasional small patch of green suggests that photosynthesis has not yet come to a complete halt, but it is a last dying effort before the tree goes into dormancy for the winter months.

Many waterfowl that breed in the far north are moving southward in November. In particular, the three species of scoter—common, surf, and white-winged—are often in large concentrations off Montauk and Orient points. Their main food here is the blue mussel, for which they dive to depths of twenty feet or more, propelling themselves underwater with their feet and steering with their wings. They swallow the mussels whole, grinding the shells up with muscular contractions of the gizzard. The grinding power of this organ is remarkable: An oyster shell, which requires a hard hammer blow to break, is easily crushed into small fragments that are ejected from the scoter's bill.

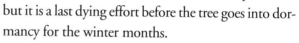

Common, Surf, and White-winged Scoters (left to right)

High-bush cranberries are now ripe, hanging in rich clusters, ready for the cedar waxwings, for which they seem to be a favorite. Low-lipid fruits like these are less susceptible to rotting and therefore persist well into the winter.

The short-eared owl, also known as the marsh owl, frequents open grasslands, dunes, and salt marshes, where it hunts for its main prey, the meadow vole. The owl hunts during the day as well as at night, so look for it on a winter's day as it tirelessly searches for its prey. Its flight is buoyant and almost mothlike, the wing beats very deep on the downstroke. The owl quarters the ground from a level of a few feet and then strikes with talons thrust forward.

When there is a population explosion of voles, which occurs every few years, the owl will produce more than one brood. The ground nest is usually in a depression in tall weeds, and as many as seven eggs are laid. Because the bird starts incubating after the first egg is laid, the chicks are of different sizes, and if the adults are unable to provide enough food for the entire brood, the older ones will devour their smaller siblings.

American holly is now bearing ripened red berries, which are a great favorite with mockingbirds and robins. The evergreen leaves, larger and not as glossy as those of the European species, stay on the plant for three years. The white, fine-grained wood takes a very high polish and is often used to make piano, organ, and accordion keys. Many small holly trees can be found in the woods near Montauk Point. And in a depression between the dunes known as Sunken Forest, near Point-O'-Woods on the barrier beach, there is a splendid grove of fine old hollies that have developed sizeable gnarled trunks. Standing in the gloom and quiet of this magical place, it is difficult to realize that the Atlantic Ocean is pounding the shoreline a very short distance away. Fortunately, the Sunken Forest is now a permanent preserve as part of the Fire Island National Seashore.

Although there has been no nesting colony of great blue herons on Long Island since 1900 (on Gardiners Island), a fair number of them winter here, forced by frozen waters in the north to seek open water farther south. They fish in brackish creeks, freshwater ponds, and salt bays and marshes. A fishing heron is the very model of patience, standing motionless in the shallows, waiting for that critical fraction of a second in which to lunge and transfix its prey with that formidable javelin of a bill. In addition to fish, this heron eats frogs, small mammals, snakes, small birds, and even insects.

The sighting of a snowy owl in the dunes on the barrier beach suggests that this might be a winter when this large, magnificent Arctic owl moves south in considerable numbers. These population explosions occur when there is a decline in the lemming population in the Arctic tundra, forcing the owls to seek other food prey, including rabbits and bay ducks, which the owls hunt in daylight. Younger individuals, the ones most likely to visit Long Island, are heavily marked with spots and bars, but the older birds are almost pure white.

The hardy red-breasted merganser appears in large flocks in our salt bays, Long Island Sound, and off the Montauk Point area. Unlike other members of the waterfowl group, mergansers have long, slender bills with serrations like tiny teeth along the edges of the mandibles to help the bird get a firm grip on its slippery prey. Sometimes these birds cooperate by forming a line abreast and driving a school of bait-fish into the shallows, where they can be caught more easily. The male and female differ greatly in plumage, but neither has a truly red breast. The handsome male has a narrow orange-brown band on the breast, and the female has a reddish-brown head, gray back, and white underparts.

Of the many species of wood warbler we see during the spring migration, one, the yellow-rumped warbler, is one of the earliest to arrive on Long Island and also the most abundant. In the fall it is one of the latest to leave, and surprisingly, many individuals remain here all winter. Unlike most of the other warbler species, this bird can readily adapt to a vegetarian diet when insects are unavailable, and small groups of them can be seen in brushy areas feeding on the berries of bayberry, sumac, and poison ivy. One of their favorite overwintering grounds is the depressions in the beach dunes. Although their winter plumage is somewhat drab compared to the striking spring finery, both sexes retain the distinctive yellow rump patch. The descriptive name for this warbler was first given to it by John James Audubon, but was later changed to myrtle warbler because of the bird's fondness for the berries of the wax myrtle in the South. Only recently has its name been officially changed back to the one bestowed on it by Audubon.

The beautifully woven nest of the northern oriole, well hidden while the leaves were on the trees, is now exposed. Usually built at the end of a drooping branch, the nest is slung by the rim between two twigs. Plant fibers, moss, strands of string, animal hair, fine grasses, and grapevine bark are all intertwined into a neat, purselike structure so well

constructed it can survive winter storms. The nest is entirely the work of the female, who receives encouragement from her mate by means of his rich, deep-whistled song.

When northern lakes become icebound, loons must move southward to open water and are content to adopt the open ocean as their winter habitat. Two species, the common and red-throated, can be seen on Long Island Sound, off Montauk Point, and along the South Shore during the colder months, but they may be harder to pick out in their drab winter plumages. The bill of the red-throated loon is slightly tilted up.

The loon is beautifully designed as a fish-catching organism: The body is torpedo-shaped, the legs with their powerful webbed feet are set far back on the body, and the strong bill is daggerlike. The bird can remain submerged for as much as three minutes and can reach depths of two hundred feet. Its outer plumage overlays a densely packed down that gives it perfect insulation against the bitter cold of the wintry seas. But to have this impressive efficiency in the water, the loon must make some sacrifices: On land, handicapped by the placement of its legs, the bird must slide on its belly and is unable to take off. On the water it needs a long runway to take off, and once airborne, it must beat its small wings very rapidly.

Sadly, these magnificent birds, so much the spirit of our northern lakes, are rapidly declining in number, partly because of disturbance by the ubiquitous outboard motorboats in the lakes where they breed, but also because of oil dumped from tankers. While wintering off our coasts, the loon comes in contact with drifting globules of heavy

Common (left) and Red-throated Loons, winter

Red-breasted Nuthatch

oil, and its feathers become so matted that cold penetrates to the body. The bird then tries to reach the shore, where it perishes slowly from pneumonia and starvation or is killed by a fox or raccoon. Or possibly it is poisoned by ingesting the oil while attempting to preen itself. Whatever the cause of death, its fate is sealed once it contacts that illegally dumped oil. A naturalist walking our winter beaches will often find the carcasses of luckless loons and other seagoing birds, victims of man's disregard for the fellow creatures with which he shares this earth.

Although there are only a few records of the red-breasted nuthatch nesting on Long Island, in some winters this lively northern species occurs here in considerable numbers, joining with loose flocks of chickadees, brown creepers, downy woodpeckers, and kinglets as they forage through the woods. This squat little bird prefers pines and other coniferous trees, as it is fond of cone seeds. And, like its close relative, the larger white-breasted nuthatch, it often climbs down the trunk of a tree rather than up as it hunts for insects and spiders in the crevices of the bark. Its call is a nasal, unbirdlike "ank."

One of our most popular winter visitors from the north is the dark-eyed junco, lovingly known as "snowbird" by country folk. This gray and white member of the sparrow family always seems to be cheerful; even a heavy snowfall brings its benefits, making it easier for the juncos to reach the seeds at the tops of weed heads. All the while the birds maintain contact with each other by their sharp "chipping" calls. Toward the end of the winter, the notes begin to run together into a kind of trill, and eventually a musical twitter indicates that the mating season is imminent, and the birds depart for the north.

Wood Duck, male, right

That Beau Brummell of the world's waterfowl, the drake wood duck, begins courtship and pair formation in the late fall. He has shed his relatively dull postnuptial plumage and is resplendent in glorious markings that include all the colors in the spectrum. In the early 1900s, this beautiful duck was in danger of extinction from being overhunted, both for its feathers and for the market. But since afforded protection, it has made a comeback and now can be found in almost any secluded woodland pond or stream. The female nests in tree cavities and can be encouraged to use nest boxes, provided they are safe from raccoons. The ducklings remain in the nest for about twenty-four hours after hatching and then, at the urging of the mother, climb to the entrance with their sharply curved claws and drop softly to the ground.

Gulls have become so abundant that it is difficult to believe that around the turn of the century naturalists were concerned about the diminishing populations of some gull species. The birds were being exploited for their feathers, and their eggs were taken for food. The great black-backed gull was a rare sight in the Northeast, and the herring gull was not in much better shape. Now, their numbers are so great that they are moving into many new habitats, including our towns and villages. As usual, man is responsible for this population imbalance. Our huge garbage dumps attract gulls by the thousands, turning the birds into large-scale scavengers. Eventually, when most garbage is recycled and the dumps are closed, it will be interesting to study how gull populations and their habits are affected.

DECEMBER

ALTHOUGH WINTER DOES NOT OFFICIALLY BEGIN until December 21, it has already announced its pending arrival with frosts, snow flurries, bare trees, frozen ground, and a skim of ice on the ponds. Our wintering land birds are availing themselves of the seeds and suet provided by kindhearted folk. And waterfowl, too, have settled down for the winter months at the feeding grounds around the coasts and in the salt bays. Because the bird populations are essentially stabilized for a while, this is the best time of year for the annual bird count organized by the National Audubon Society. The Christmas bird count has been conducted annually since 1900, and by comparing the data from the many counts, we can learn a great deal about trends in bird populations.

One bird that is very erratic in its visitations to Long Island during the winter is the evening grosbeak. In some years, dozens of them are at the feeders, squabbling and gorging on sunflower seeds. In other years, not a single one is seen. There is a correlation between the abundance of pine cone seeds in the northern forests and the wanderings of this species: If the cones are plentiful, the birds do not leave their summer homes, but if there is a failure in the crop, they move southward to seek alternative food resources. They are strikingly handsome in their black, white, and gold plumage, and we welcome them at our feeders in spite of the enormous inroads they make into our sunflower seed supplies.

One of the thrills for winter waterfowl watchers is sighting a gorgeous little drake harlequin duck. This species is never abundant and usually occurs as a pair or small group of individuals. In the north, the harlequins are known as the "lords and ladies of the waters," but in truth only the male displays courtly trappings; the striking markings of the drake are in sharp contrast to the drab hen, whose whitish spots on the side of the head distinguish her from the hen bufflehead.

In the far north where they breed, harlequins nest near swiftly running streams. In their winter territory, they are usually seen close to rocks. The Montauk Point area and the inlets along the South Shore around the rock jetties are good spots to look for them. They feed almost entirely on aquatic animal matter, including chitons, or coat-of-mail shells. How they are able to pry these creatures from the rocks, where they are securely attached by powerful suction pads, is an unsolved puzzle.

Small groups of common eider, traveling in long, irregular lines over the water, have now joined the large flocks of scoters wintering off Montauk and Orient points. A few king eiders are also occasionally seen. Although the females of the two species are difficult to tell apart, the male king is readily identified by its black back and bright-orange frontal plate to the bill. Off our coasts the principal food of the eider is the blue mussel, which is taken from the sea bottom at depths of up to fifty feet and swallowed whole, its shell broken up by the powerful contractions of the eider's gizzard.

The handsome, hardy eider is noted commercially for its down. The brown-plumaged female plucks the down from her breast to line her nest and to serve as a cover for the eggs when she is not incubating them. The down, one of the best heat-insulating materials known, is particularly valuable for lightweight sleeping bags and polar clothing. In their breeding range in Iceland, Norway, and parts of Canada, the birds are given full protection and become almost as tame as barnyard ducks. When the down is care-

Common Eider, male, left

fully removed from the nest, the female plucks her breast again. Because the collecting of the down does not affect the eider's reproductive success, this is an excellent example of the sensible use of a valuable natural resource.

Locally, the black duck is a bird of the salt marshes as well as brackish streams and ponds. In the winter it gathers in large flocks in the salt bays. Although it is closely related to the mallard, the two have very different temperaments: The mallard readily adapts to humans and becomes semidomesticated with little encouragement, whereas the black duck is always wary, alert, and distrustful of man and can seldom be domesticated. Hunters find the black duck difficult to lure to decoys, as it has extraordinarily keen eyesight, and the slightest movement in the blind sends it out of range in a flash. When flushed, it makes a powerful upward spring, rising perpendicularly ten feet or more before starting on its swift, direct flight. Although its body is a dusky brown, the undersides of the wings are a gleaming silvery white, a good field mark even at a long distance.

Unlike the mallard, which inhabits almost the entire Northern Hemisphere, the black duck is confined to the eastern and central areas of North America. Recently, its populations have decreased alarmingly, perhaps because of pressures from the more adaptable mallard. Certainly, the northeastern mallard population has increased remarkably in recent years.

The horned lark—whose "horns" are merely tufts of tiny feathers—seems to prefer open, barren-looking wastes rather than areas with lush grass and weeds. A few can generally be found wintering among the sand dunes on the barrier beach, and considerable numbers are attracted to fields where potatoes and other crops have been harvested. The birds flock closely together, walking swiftly on their short legs, gleaning seeds as they go, occasionally flushing and wheeling about in the air before settling down again to feed. Like the longspurs, pipits, and other birds frequenting open, windswept areas, the horned lark has exceptionally long claws on its hind toes, probably to give this hardy little bird additional support when it faces into the winter gales. As a further testimonial to this bird's hardiness, it can sometimes be seen enjoying a snow bath.

The rough-legged hawk is a winter visitor to our area, having been forced south from its breeding range in the Arctic and sub-Arctic by adverse weather. It hunts over open fields, dunes, and marshes, seeking with its remarkably keen eyes the voles, mice, and rabbits that are its main prey. Sometimes it hovers over one spot, extending its talons in preparation for a strike. Large and slow, the rough-legged hawk is often a target for the thoughtless and uneducated hunter; in view of its usefulness to the farmer, it deserves maximum protection.

Privet, introduced into the United States from Europe many years ago, is doing well in its adopted home, producing thick hedges where needed, and in many areas going wild. The small purplish-black berries are excellent food for birds; the bobwhite, in particular, is fond of them.

What is this? Swallows here in midwinter? Surely not. But it is indeed so. The tree swallow has learned to adapt to a vegetarian diet during the colder months, and some remain among the South Shore dunes, where the berries of poison ivy and the bayberry enable them to survive. Other members of the swallow family must travel thousands of miles to overwinter in tropical America.

The brilliant crimson of the fall foliage of staghorn sumac has passed, but we still have the rich deep-red, cone-shaped clusters of tiny seeds, each covered with a fuzzy coat. These fruits are a source of food for many songbirds. If you moisten the palm of your hand, rub it over a fruit cluster, and then lick your palm, you'll discover a pleasant lemonade taste. This handsome shrub gets its name from the branches, which bear a striking resemblance to deer antlers "in velvet."

The leaves of most ferns wither and die back to the rootstock during the colder months, but the Christmas fern stays fresh and green all year round. At Christmastime, brush aside the snow to reveal the glossy, deep green leaves.

With a broad stretch of imagination, you might see the shape of a Christmas stocking in each little leaflet. Look for the Christmas fern where there is stony soil and some tree shade.

Two particularly attractive winter visitors from the far north are the fox and tree sparrows. The fox is our largest sparrow, and as its name indicates it has much foxy-red in its plumage. In its search for seeds and insects, this bird can create quite a commotion by its habit of scratching in the dead

Tree Sparrow   *Fox Sparrow*

leaves, leaping into the air as it kicks with its powerful feet. The tree sparrow is definitely misnamed, for it spends most of its life on or near the ground and does not even nest in trees in its breeding range in northern Canada and Newfoundland. Small flocks of this hardy bird can be seen feeding on the seeds from weed heads in the midst of a driving snowstorm, giving their tinkling, bell-like songs with every suggestion of cheerfulness. The dusky spot on the unstreaked breast is a good field mark.

The Christmas bird count has already been mentioned, but it is worth describing in more detail because it is considered by many ornithologists, both amateur and professional, to be the premier birding event of the year. Initiated in 1900 by a small group of enthusiasts, it has been held annually ever since; now more than fifteen hundred communities all over North America, and some in Central and South America and Hawaii, participate. In 1984 more than forty thousand birders counted about 109 million birds of more than six hundred species. The surveys are carefully checked and reported to the National Audubon Society, which publishes them in the *Journal of American Birds*.

Each group of birders covers a prescribed fifteen-mile-diameter circle on a day around Christmas Day, counting every bird that can be positively identified, with always the hope of spotting some exciting, record-breaking rarity. Obviously, areas in southern regions produce counts of far more birds than those in the frozen north—a group in the Republic of Panama counted 311 different species one year, while counters in upper Quebec could find only three species—but all reports are of value in indicating population fluctuations, shifts of ranges, food availability, and migration phenomena. However many or however few are counted, it is a fun and healthy activity for all participants, as well as being of considerable scientific value. It is a time for being with good friends and for sharpening up bird-identification skills. The day usually ends with a gathering where all can recount their finds in an atmosphere of satisfaction and relaxation.

AFTERWORD

WE'VE REACHED THE END OF THE YEAR in this random collection of happenings in Long Island's natural world, but for Nature it is not the end at all. Time flows on into the new year, and the cycle of life also continues, unimpeded by man's arbitrary spans of time, whether years, seasons, months, weeks, or days.

We are all, to some extent, aware of this flow of life, and many of us take delight in observing details of the grand pattern: the first greening of a grass blade, the tentative notes in the start of a robin's song, the rich pink tip of a budding apple blossom, the first touch of orange in a fall maple leaf, a dusting of white frost in a hollow in the lawn—these all move us gently from one phase to the next.

Long Island is a splendid stage in which to observe the cyclical pattern. It is, in some ways, a discrete geographical and ecological entity, and its diverse ecosystems provide endless fascination: the open ocean, barrier beaches, salt bays, salt marshes, deciduous woods, old fields, freshwater ponds and streams, farmlands, meadows—everything but mountains. And because Long Island lies in the overlap between two major life zones, we have birds, and the habitats they need, from the north as well as touches of the south in the piney woods and some of our swamplands.

Sadly, Long Island is too close to the great metropolis for its own good; it is becoming Manhattan's bedroom more and more as developments inexorably gobble up open land. Many environmental groups are battling to preserve what is left, and they are putting up a magnificent fight. The Nature Conservancy, the local chapters of the National Audubon Society, the Pine Barrens Society, the Greenbelt, and many more are dedicated to the selfless effort of saving the best of Long Island for future generations.

And it was here, in 1967, that we saw the birth of one of the most important environmental groups of all, the Environmental Defense Fund. As the coal miners' canary in times past warned the miners of the presence of deadly methane gas, the decline of the osprey in the 1960s (see March) warned us that something was wrong in our environment. In a lawsuit heard in the New York State Supreme Court, the judge was convinced by scientific testimony that the DDT used to control mosquitoes in Suffolk County was adversely affecting many non-target organisms as well—ospreys, blueclaw crabs, and bay fish among others. The use of DDT was stopped, and from this humble beginning on Long Island, the Environmental Defense Fund was founded, going on to become a powerful force for environmental protection with worldwide concerns. While acid rain, global warming, and the depletion of the earth's ozone layer are all on its docket, the Environmental Defense Fund is still involved in Long Island's environmental struggles.

There are many battles waiting for us in the coming years, some we are still unaware of. But our canaries, be they osprey, crab, fish, polluted streams, filled-in marshes, or other signals, are there to warn us of environmental threats, and we must pay full attention to these warnings. Long Island has much to offer through its natural wonders, and we must work together to give it the protection, the respect, and yes, the love that is its due.

INDEX